AMUKAH
THE HIDDEN VALLEY

MORDECHAI MENACHEM REICH

Copyright © 1992 by Mordechai Menachem Reich
Kiryat Meor Chaim 6/78, Tzfas, Israel

All rights reserved.
This book, or any part thereof,
may not be reproduced in any
form whatsoever without the express
written permission of the copyright holder.

A TORASTAR PUBLICATION

ISBN 1-56062-078-129-X

Printed by Gross Brothers Printing Co.
Union City, New Jersey, U.S.A.

Table of Contents

Chapter One: **Journey to Meiron** 1

Chapter Two: **Eventful Night in Meiron** 15

Chapter Three: **Attempt to Amukah** 25

Chapter Four: **Kissei Eliyahu** 31

Chapter Five: **A Good Night's Sleep** 43

Chapter Six: **Setting Out To Amukah** 57

Chapter Seven: **Unbearable Thirst** 65

Chapter Eight: **Lost in the Forest** 77

Chapter Nine: **On the Right Path** 83

Chapter Ten: **Amukah at Last!** 87

Chapter Eleven: **Tzefas** 93

Chapter Twelve: **Back to Yerushalayim** 103

Chapter Thirteen: **The Phone Call** 109

Chapter Fourteen: **Trans-Atlantic Search** 127

Chapter Fifteen: **The Lesson of Amukah** 137

Chapter Sixteen: **The Dream** 141

Chapter Seventeen: **Settling Down Near Amukah** 145

Chapter One

Journey to Meiron

I had first heard of Amukah while studying at the Institute of Advanced Talmudic study in Lakewood, New Jersey. Many of my colleagues talked of the miracles and wonders that could be achieved there by the utterance of but a single earnest prayer.

Amukah, which means 'deep valley' is actually that, a deep valley nestled in a desolate hidden expanse of the Galilean forest situated between the holy city of Tzefas and the ancient historical city of Hatzor. Amukah is the holy eternal resting place of the Tanna, R. Yonoson ben Uziel. It is said of the holy Tanna that he himself assured heaven's speedy salvation to anyone taking the courage and effort to embark upon the difficult journey to his hidden resting place. Indeed his assurance could be as good as guaranteed, for the strength of R. Yonoson leaped above and beyond the physical bounds of mortal men. An example of his holiness and sanctity is vividly portrayed by the Talmud (Succah 28a): "When R. Yonoson ben Uziel studied Torah, any bird flying over his head would be instantly burnt, so intense was the fire of his holiness when he studied Hashem's fiery Law." His greatness is further demonstrated by his completion of a precise translation and indepth commentary on the entire Books of Prophets which also revealed many hidden divine secrets. The Land of Israel quaked at his revelations and the heavens declared, "Who is the one who dared to reveal My secrets to man of flesh and blood?" "O Master of the universe, great and omnipotent King, it is I who has done this, but it is revealed before Thee, O great King, that not for my honor, or for that of my father's honor did I do this, but to avoid conflict and strife amongst your children, so that the true meaning of the text be clearly understood and not ambiguous for ambiguity would cause much strife and dissension amongst the students and scholars of Torah." Hashem was pleased with his explanation.

Seeing that he had found favor in Hashem's eyes, R. Yonoson commenced a new work; his commentary of the Scriptures, a holy undertaking in the dissemination of Hashem's true and unambiguous intentions to mankind. It was not to be. "A heavenly voice rang out from above in stark declaration: Enough!" The secrets contained in the Scriptures would not be allowed to be revealed to the public. They would have to remain concealed. What was so special about the secrets contained therein? Rashi commentates: "It refers to the Book of Daniel wherein lies the exact moment of Messiah's coming and Israel's final redemption."

Understandably, it would be detrimental to reveal such information and would therefore obviously have to remain hidden, as hidden a R. Yonoson's grave would be in the hidden valley of Amukah.

The holy Tanna obediently desisted from writing the commentary, and continued his tireless and joyous study of Torah and performance of *mitzvos*. But let us just imagine this. R. Yonoson could have actually revealed to mankind his quest for the knowledge of the Messiah's coming and Israel's final redemption from the servitude of her longest, darkest and bitterest exile. A powerful giant entrusted with this secret had to be able to perform miracles in the form of interceding upon the behalf of those whose broken-hearted souls beckoned them to approach his holy grave in earnest prayer.

A young man searching for his bride to be, his partner in life eternal, was promised his mate speedily from heaven, if he would but utter a heart rending and tearful prayer at R. Yonoson's grave. My heart throbbed, and an inner voice prodded my yearning to travel to Amukah, as I was very much still searching for mine. The fact that my dearest friend, a brother to me, four years my junior, had just gotten unofficially engaged, compounded that yearning. I was elated at the good news about his good find; I was ecstatic that he had found his help mate. Still, I couldn't help feeling somewhat like a man standing all alone at a dock watching his best friend's ship sail off into the distance, towards opportunity, that is, married life. I had to move. Travel. Get my mind off the pain.

And so on a Sunday, Erev Rosh Chodesh Elul, the day when my friend's unofficially engaged bride to be was to speak with her father long distance for his official blessing, I proceeded to my apartment on Rechov Malachi packed some things for my trip to the north, and boarded a local bus to the Central Bus Station. At the station, I inquired about the route schedule to Meiron. I had heard that many visited R. Shimon's gravesite on Rosh Chodesh Elul, for great things could be achieved there at precisely this time through prayer and Torah study. I had planned an itinerary comprising several holy *kevarim*, where I would pour out my heart in prayer. Meiron would be most appropriately first on that itinerary. After this, I would, with the help of Hashem, embark upon the difficult journey to R. Yonoson ben Uziel's gravesite to Amukah, the climax of my efforts.

After I had gotten the proper bus route schedule information, I proceeded to the end of a long line of patiently waiting prospective travelers, and anxiously anticipated the bus' arrival.

The transit information representative had informed me that there was no direct bus to Meiron available. I would have to therefore take a bus to Teverya and change there for a bus to Meiron via Tzefas.

At about five o'clock the bus arrived and everyone filed on. As the bus closed its doors and pulled away from the station, I noticed that the sun was beginning to set. The driver turned right, onto Rechov Yirmiyahu and continued down Bar Ilan, Yirmiyahu's exention, till the Ramat Eshkol-Sanhedria junction. There, he turned right onto Rechov Shmuel HaNavi and continued down that street until he reached the Rechov Shaar Shechem intersection. Turning left, he proceeded towards Shaar Shechem. Once there he turned left again and traveled adjacent to the Old City walls till he reached the Mount of Olives. *Har Hazeisim*, my beloved father's eternal resting place, stood majestically before me.

As the bus climbed upwards, I noticed the Temple walls and the gold and silver domes on the *Har Habayis*, to my right. Up, the bus climbed, past the entrance gate to my father's *chelka* (grave plot section), as I strained to catch a glimpse of his holy resting place. To my frustration, visual obstructions denied me the opportunity, but as the bus veered left round the curve, I was relieved to notice that my father's *tzion* would be coming into full view momentarily. As we reached the point of the road directly opposite my father's *chelka*, my eyes searched for a glimpse of it. Yes, for a fleeting second, I caught sight of it, and my lips offered a silent prayer. My heart prayed: "Dear beloved father whom I miss so much, I am now on my way to the north, to pray at the *mekomos hakedoshim*. Tatti, you are in heaven closer to the Heavenly Throne and Hashem Yisborach, than I am here on this world. Please be a *'meilitz yosher'* for me, plead my case if you can, that I should merit my *zivug* very soon. *Techiyas hasmeisim* will transpire in the near future and we will be reunited forever. I cannot wait to see you, to be with you to have our long conversations, as we used to have not so long ago." Not so long ago indeed, as it was only a year and a half since Hashem Yisborach had taken him from me.

As I finished my emotional prayer, I turned round to catch a last glimpse of the silver dome and the walls of the Holy Temple, with the intent of sending my prayer upwards through the gate of Heaven, located directly above the Holy Temple Mount. The Torah attests to this gate in the travels of Jacob: "And he said, 'for this is the gate of Heaven.'" The Midrash elucidates that all prayer transcends this world towards heaven, through this gate, and the Me'am Lo'ez comments, "Worthy is he who merits to pray at the Western Wall, for his prayer ascends directly to heaven, through this gate of all prayers." The Midrash continues to say, that people around the world, must rely upon the angels to hear, accept, and bring their prayers to this gate, but those who merit to pray here by the Wall of the Temple, have the good fortune in that Hashem Himself collects the supplications of the broken hearted, and personally takes them to His Heavenly Throne.

I caught sight of the Holy Mountain and the Temple walls for a fleeting second as the bus veered round a curve, just long enough to hurl my prayer by the agent of my eyes, towards the heavenly gate, where Hashem Himself was anxiously awaiting with open arms, to accept my heart rending supplication.

I turned back towards my father's *chelka* with the hope of catching one last glimpse in order to solidify and combine his eternal resting place with that of the Holy Temple Mount, through the catalyst of my prayer. Having succeeded in doing that, I noted that I had started my trip by praying at the first *makom kadosh*, my father's gravesite. I settled back in my seat with that interesting and comforting thought, breathed a deep sigh of relief and turned my attention to the itinerary of the coming trip.

Would I find solace and comfort at Meiron? How many pilgrims would be present there praying and studying? Would I succeed in obtaining lodging for the night? What about food and drink? After all, I had never done this before; setting out in the evening towards a place, not knowing where I would lay my head down for the night or how I would sustain myself. Nevertheless, these doubts dissipated as quickly as they had formed, for my *bitachon* in Hashem Yisborach transcended all doubt. I felt that Hashem Himself was holding me in His arms, protecting me from peril and danger. Where was I going? Where would I stay? Avraham Avinu gathered his belongings and traveled, no questions, no doubts, for he knew Hashem and trusted in Him. "Travel the land; sojourn in it." I felt, somehow, that this command was intended for me too. "Have no doubts, my beloved son. This holy land is your land. Feel free, and above all, safe to walk in the land of your forefathers." This resounding voice, penetrating the innermost chambers of my conscience, reassured me that all would be taken care of, for "Hashems' eyes are upon this holy land from the beginning of the year to the end of the year."

And a most beautiful land for one to lay his eyes upon indeed, I noticed, scanning the picturesque landscape from the bus' large and spacious panorama windows.

The bus slowly rounded the sharp curves of East Yerushalayim and approached the new settlement of Maalei Adumim. Maalei Adumim, the 'Red Heights' appeared on our right, its rich soil bursting forth with a fiery red color hue, reflecting the setting sun's splendorous and brilliant red orange rays.

We sped past Maalei Adumim, and the road had straightened out before us. We were fast approaching the Judean desert. The sun's last rays gently bathed the smooth desert sand dunes, portraying the hills as a quiet ocean, its waves stilled by the serene atmosphere brought on by the inevitable dusk.

As we entered the desert, a forboding, arid, desolate expanse, a seemingly G-d forsaken habitat, void of water, vegetation and in effect void of life, I could not help but shudder at the frightening thought of being stranded out there alone to fend for survival. It felt good, rather reassuring to be inside the bus. I felt comfortable and secure to have the people sitting all around me, as if we were in this together, braving the ominous and forboding desert.

We began descending towards the Dead Sea, Jordan Valley basin, rather rapidly and I found myself adjusting to the drastic altitude differentiation in air pressure by swallowing intermittently. About thirty minutes later we emerged from the desert hills and moved along toward the vast wide open spaces of the Jordan Valley plain. I could faintly make out the northernmost tip of the Dead Sea, where it met the sweet waters of the Jordan River. Several minutes passed and the bus stopped at the Jericho junction to discharge soldiers. As we started up again, I noticed that the bus was readying to turn left, and I was excited, for it meant that we would be following the direction of the sign before us which pointed towards the oldest and lowest city on the face of the earth, the biblical city of Jericho!

I had travelled the Yerushalayim-Dead Sea highway many times before, but never had I come upon the opportunity to turn left at the Jericho junction. I had always continued straight ahead to the Dead Sea, and south along its shores, toward Qumran, Ein Fashca, Ein Kalya, Ein Gedi and Massada. Now would be the first time I would be turning off at the junction towards the north. I was thrilled with anticipation.

The last time I had travelled to the north (the first time in my life, and also by myself), I had taken the train from Yerushalayim to Haifa via the West coast, hence I had never toured the Jordan Valley, popularly known as the 'west bank' and therefore had never seen Jericho. This famous and important historical biblical city, the first in the holy land to be conquered by Joshua and the Israelites after having crossed the Jordan River, lay before me. I could barely make out the faint outline of the numerous palm trees in the distance, owing to the setting sun which had already dipped over the horizon.

'City of Palm Trees' as Jericho is frequently referred to, is an apropo and exact description of the ancient city, for it is so densely populated with palm trees, that a natural oasis attributing complete shade over the entire city, prevails. A green canopy of beautiful foliage stretches over the entire city and its environs, protecting her from the intense broiling heat of the Middle Eastern midday scorching sun. I recall another time, later on, traveling through this area during the month of February. I had left Yerushalayim wearing a wool sweater and a heavy winter coat, but when the bus reached the Jordan Valley plain, the sudden heat became unbearable. Everyone removed their winter coats and sweaters, and opened the windows wide, and still it was uncomfortably warm, so you can well imagine how unbearably hot the climate can get during the scorching summer months and the obvious benefit to be derived from the shade of the palm trees.

As evening had approached, and night was quickly falling, the windows of the bus were wide open allowing the gentle desert breeze in, bringing a brisk zest of fresh air to all.

As we got closer to Jericho, I took note of the innumerous palm trees congested and concentrated everywhere. What a sight to behold!

When we entered the city proper, we were plunged into complete darkness, owing to the shade caused by the numerous palm trees which lined the main street. The bus driver put on his vehicle lights, and was guided by them to the main market street. Once there, the many gaily lit lanterns, which were hung over the wares of oranges and grapefruits in the market stores, lit up the area. The bright orange and yellow colors of the citrus were tempting indeed, asthetically arranged for the consumer's eye.

The residents of Jericho sat at their cafes' sipping Turkish coffee, wiling away the evening hours in relaxation. Everything was so clean and orderly, from the neatly arranged citrus to the neatly attired residents. A sense of absolute calm prevailed throughout. Even the donkeys, I noticed, moved comfortably along under their bundles of fruit and spices, led by their masters dressed in spanking white cotton, which contrasted with their vibrant and healthy looking olive skin.

So this is the city the Prophets called 'Ir Hatamarim,' 'The city of the palm trees.' Yes, of course, for as a matter of fact, most of the *lulavim* used by religious observant Jews throughout the world during the Succos festival still come to this very day from this ancient biblical city.

Fifteen minutes elapsed and the tour of Jericho was over. As we left the city I noticed that the stars had come out. I laid my head back on the head rest and caught a nap. When I awoke, I glanced at my watch, and noticed it was seven o'clock. About another hour and a half to go. I began thinking about the recent events, my best friend's engagement, and the situation in general. The bus was speeding northward, curving up and down the west bank hills. I looked out the window to my right and noticed a cluster of twinkling lights in the far off distance. I inquired of my seat mate about them and he informed me that we were looking at a village situated on the east bank of the Jordan River, in the country of Jordan! That was a shock to me. "You mean we are so close to Jordan?" I exclaimed. "Yes," he replied. As a matter of fact," he continued, "we are less than a mile away from the Jordan River itself, which is the border between us." I shuddered at the thought of it. "Isn't it dangerous to be traveling out here at night, so close to the border?" I asked.

"Many people prefer to travel the east coast, via Tel Aviv and Haifa, to the north, over this dark and curvy second class road near the border," he stated.

I took a chance taking this bus, but I figured that there was not that much really to worry about since there would still be plenty of traffic on the road till about nine o'clock. Besides, taking a bus from Yerushalayim to Haifa and from Haifa to Teverya, would have been like scratching my right ear with my left hand. For those traveling from Tel Aviv, the Haifa connection towards Teverya would be logical owing to its geographical location. But from Yerushalayim, the best, shortest, and therefore fastest way to Teverya would be via Jericho and the west bank of the Jordan Valley. "We should be getting into Teverya about eight-fifteen or eigh-thirty. It should be ok," he said.

I thanked him kindly for his assurance, and shot a quick glance at my wristwatch. It was seven thirty. About an hour left to go. We pulled into Bet She'an for a quick ten minute stop and were off again.

At about eight, the glistening waters of the Kinneret appeared suddenly before me as if out of nowhere. The trees and dense brush at the water's edge, concealed the lake's shore and therefore it was suddenly that I found myself traveling along the water's edge toward the coastal city of Teverya. What a beautiful sight indeed. The shimmering waves gently rippling towards the sandy shore, reflected the moon's silvery rays, giving the lake a mystical aura.

As we neared our destination, I caught sight of the white dome over R. Meir Baal Haness' *kever*, off the road to our left. We sped by it and several minutes later approached the environs of Teverya. At about eight-twenty we pulled into the deserted Central Bus Station.

This was the last stop on the line and everybody disembarked. Now I had to concern myself with catching a bus to Meiron via Tzefas. I noticed two yeshiva boys who had gotten off the bus with me so I approached them and inquired whether they were perhaps also traveling to Meiron.

They replied, "Yes we are, but the bus driver notified us that the last bus to Tzefas already left this station at eight o'clock."

"Then how will we get to Meiron?" I asked.

"The bus driver informed us, that the last bus to Kiryat Shemoneh will be arriving at eight-thirty. That's in about five minutes. He suggested to take that bus to Rosh Pinna, and to disembark there, near the Tzefas junction."

"And then what?"

"To hitch."

"At nine o'clock at night? Isn't it dangerous?"

"Do you have another choice?"

As I thought of a reply, the Kiryat Shemoneh bus rolled in. It stopped adjacent to us, and opened its doors. My state of indecision caused me to hesitate, but when the two yeshiva boys hopped on the bus, I looked around the totally deserted station and instinctively hopped on too. It certainly wouldn't be too comfortable standing all alone in a deserted Central Bus Station.

The bus pulled out of the *Tachana Mercazit*, traveled north along the Kinneret's shores, and then began its steep upward climb towards the majestic Galilean mountains. As we winded our way up the serpentine road, I noticed the twinkling sparkling lights of Teverya by the shore down below. What a breathtaking sight to behold! Teverya sparkled like the brilliant stars in the night. A truly beautiful and mystical fairy-tale like city, its lights glistening as crystal, pearls and diamonds shimmer against the setting of black velvet.

Up, the bus climbed, groaning under the strain of each steep turn. Upwards it groped, pulling its burdenous weight with great difficulty.

We passed the *Pnei Hamayim* (sea level) marker and continued climbing higher and higher. We were now really very high up, as the twinkling lights of Teverya down below, seemed so far away. So distant that I could hardly make them out anymore.

I swallowed several times to alleviate the differentiation in altitude pressure and noted it rather interesting to have gone from the heights of the Judean Mountains to the depths of the Dead Sea, only to ascend from the depths of the Kinneret Sea to the heights of the Galilean Mountains. From the heights to the depths, to the heights again. A person falls only to rise. An important lesson, from the holy terrain of the Land of Israel. One immerses in a mikvah to gain purification, in order to continue in his holy work. I descended to the water of the Dead Sea, Jordan River and Kinneret, and rose to embark upon my holy mission of prayer. In the land of Israel, every step of the way incorporates an inherent lesson.

The bus had leveled off now to fairly flat ground and the two yeshiva boys advised me to get ready as we were nearing the Rosh Pinna - Tzefas junction.

Five minutes later, the bus came to a stop and the driver announced, "Rosh Pinna - Tzomed Tzefas." We disembarked with our things and watched the bus pull away, towards the north, where its last stop would be Kiryat Shemoneh.

My companions and I crossed the road and took up position at the junction's designated hitchhiking spot near the sign which read Tzefas 12KM. My companions were not too pleased with my company, I sensed, since 'hitching well' assuredly meant traveling with less people. They were two, and that was hard enough. But three standing together would prove rather difficult. I felt their discomfort and immediately offered to stand aside, separate from them, explaining that I understood very well. Though embarrassed at first, they eagerly accepted my offer and explanation with a nod of understanding. I moved over several yards, looked at them and thought: nine o'clock at night, under the stars of the sky, and I'm out in the middle of nowhere, hungry and cold, anticipating the good will of a kind-hearted motorist! An adventure. More than that. An opportunity. A rare chance to come closer to Hashem. I would try the utmost to savor each and every moment of this uplifting experience and keep in mind that Hashem would be guiding me from above, every step of the way.

As I was getting drained from standing and waiting, I chose a small boulder a few yards from the sign and set my aching body down. The two fellows didn't dare chance to sit for fear of losing a speeding and impatient motorist. They stood at attention waiting to pounce on any prospective candidate, and there weren't any.

About twenty minutes later, a small white Peugot station wagon appeared, slowed down and stopped. The driver clearly and emphatically stated that there was only room for two. They pounced for the door but then hesitated, turning to look at me with a slight apparent expression of apprehension and sympathy. I nodded my approval, that it was ok and that I would get along by myself just fine, and they opened those doors faster than lightening, hopped in and were gone.

The distant drone of the car's engine could still be heard in the stillness of the night, as I lifted my eyes towards the sky and marvelled at the countless stars twinkling at me. It was as if they were saying, "We are here above, watching that nothing happens to you. Though we are silent and still, our sparkling light shall illuminate your path in the darkness of night." Actually, it was Hashem showing me that He was personally protecting me and the stars were accompanying Him as His hosts.

I glanced at my wristwatch. It was already nine forty-five. Almost five hours on the road! The strenuous trip was beginning to take its toll, as the drain on my energy was becoming more and more evident with each passing minute.

I glanced at my wrist watch again. Almost ten! Suddenly I cocked my ear as I groped to make out the faint distant murmur of a car's motor. It became clearer as the vehicle made its way closer to me. Finally, I saw it, as it rounded a curve and came into full view. Would it slow down? At least to give a 'chance look' at this poor traveler stranded, tired, cold and hungry, standing, waiting and hoping under the stars, so late at night. "Please Hashem." It began slowing down. I drew a deep sigh of relief, grabbed my attaché and rushed over to the car.

"Where to?"

"Meiron."

"Hop in."

"Thanks."

I got in and closed the door. It felt good to be in the warmth of the car. And my aching leg muscles, caressed the soft upholstery of the seat as if to say 'thanks.'

"Thank you very much."

"*Al Lo Davar* - It's nothing really."

"I've been on the road since five o'clock."

"That's a long time. Where are you coming from?"

"Yerushalayim."

"And you're going to Meiron?"

"Yes, that's right."

"What made you set out to Meiron?"

"Tonight is Rosh Chodesh Elul and many travel to Meiron to pray at this specially designated time."

"Oh, I see. Well, what happened? Why were you left stranded in the middle of the trip?"

"The last connecting bus to Meiron via Tzefas, from Teverya, had already disembarked from the Central Bus Station, before I had gotten there."

"So you took the last Kiryat Shemoneh bus to the Rosh Pinna - Tzefas junction."

"Yes."

"Will you have a place to stay?"

"I shall find a place."

"I must say, you seem to have a lot of trust in Hashem."

"It is the only choice."

Impressed at my attitude, he turned to get a good look at my face and then turned his attention back to the road. I noticed that we were traveling steeply upwards. It was a continuous climb taking us higher and higher.

"My, we are climbing very high, aren't we?" I remarked.

"Well, in order to reach Tzefas and Meiron we must keep on going higher and higher. They are way above us."

"And I thought I had reached the top, when I had disembarked at Rosh Pinna."

"As a matter of fact, Rosh Pinna is way above sea level and very high up in altitude. But Tzefas and Meiron are even more. Mount Meiron, the highest mountain in Israel proper is adjacent to Tzefas, so you can well imagine how high in altitude Tzefas and Meiron are."

"Practically very close to heaven. Maybe that's why Tzefas and Meiron were chosen to become the cities of the Kabbalists, for they are above man's earthly, mundane pursuits, closer to the perfect wisdom of heaven."

"You have an idea there."

Higher and higher we got, closer to the stars of the night sky. How sparkling clear they appeared from my open window. About ten minutes later, we leveled off.

"We are nearing Tzefas. Another five minutes or so," he assured.

I glanced at my watch. It was ten twenty-five.

We sped through Tzefas at about ten-thirty. Twelve minutes of fast curvy turns later, the driver announced, "Meiron!" I opened my door and disembarked, saying a warm thank you and good night to the hospitable driver, and he continued on his way. My watch read a quarter to eleven. Six hours on the road!

Yes, this was Meiron, but I hadn't yet actually arrived. For to reach R. Shimon's *tzion*, I would still have to walk a quarter of a mile or so, uphill all the way, and in the darkness of night no less.

As I was readying to begin my ascent, two soldiers suddenly appeared. They approached me and inquired as to where they could obtain water to quench their thirst. I suggested that they would find plenty of it at R. Shimon's *tzion*, up the hill. They declined to go up the hill and decided to continue on to Haifa. I bid them good night and began the ascent alone...(incidentally, they did ascend the hill to the *tzion* later on, where I observed them receiving plenty of food and drink. I even found them places to sleep in the same building where I would later sleep). But for now, my story continues, after I had bid them farewell at the bottom of the hill and began my ascent towards R. Shimon's *tzion* alone.

I began the steep climb at a brisk pace, in the hope of getting it over with, but half way up, I had to slow down. I couldn't take the strain. The slow pace, slowed even more, to a turtle's crawl. Had I forgotten that I hadn't eaten or rested in the past six hours? My legs reminded me of these facts. I practically dragged myself up the remaining way. Finally, the *tzion* came into view and it was a genuine relief to have actually arrived.

Chapter Two

Eventful Night in Meiron

R. Shimon's *tzion* was not more than a hundred yard's away. The building was lit up with bright lights in contrast to the pitch black darkness of the night.

Makeshift tents and the aroma of food permeated the air. Along both sides of the road, I observed tents with people in them, eating, playing musical instruments or just having conversation. The tempting smell of roasted meat was tantalizing. I was famished. But was it kosher? And there were other luscious foods and plenty of drink. I licked my lips in desperation. I was hungry, yet too ashamed, too bashful, to ask for a helping. I contained myself in desperation. Maybe some kind-hearted person would approach me and offer some of his kosher delicacies, which would spare me the agony of having to ask. Of course, it would have to be a religious person, as I would not even dare to touch a morsel of unkosher food.

As I entered the courtyard of the Holy *tzion* I noticed a sign above the entrance gate which read, "How terribly and frighteningly holy is this place!" Indeed, for the holy angel, the author of the Zohar, in all his illustrious glory, was at rest here at this very spot. The spirit of this man of miracles and immeasurable spiritual strength, hovered over this very shrine.

In the courtyard, there were dozens of women sitting on the stone floor, with large platters of kushus on their laps. They were wearing the traditional Morrocan, Tunisian, head kerchiefs and were murmuring prayers with their eyes turned heavenward. Holy women. Truly G-d fearing. It inspired me.

I asked a young man, what it was all about and why the tents were put up around the area. He explained that the Sefardim came every year at L'ag B'omer and Erev Rosh Chodesh Elul, put up tents and stayed sometimes a full week, to pray at R. Shimon's *tzion*. Much food was brought from home and even more prepared on the spot, for the purpose of giving much of it away to hungry pilgrims. In doing this charitable deed, they hoped to gain atonement through R. Shimon's intervention in Heaven. That's why the women had these food platters on their legs. Some of them had gotten up and began offering handsome helpings of seminola, vegetables and cubes of luscious succulent meat, 'cuscus' as the Morrocans call it, to the hungry pilgrims.

A woman approached me and began scooping up a generous portion with a large ladle, but I had to politely decline. How was the animal slaughtered? Was it broiled in the fire long enough to remove every last drop of blood? Were the vegetables tithed *k'halacha*? It took a lot of strength, fortitude and will to abstain from enjoying a scrumptious meal, especially when I saw so many partaking of the delicacies. O, the pain. My stomach began growling for food. I noticed that the woman had kosher wafers and *petel* (a Koolaid drink), so I politely asked her for some. She quickly gave me a whole bunch and a few drinks with a big and warm smile. That saved me. I felt a sudden surge of energy and alertness permeate my being.

I guess I was so over tired, that my exhaustion suddenly just dissipated. Like passing the border limit, to a second wind. It's the feeling you have when you're so tired and then unexpectedly, you pass the extreme line and suddenly feel rejuvenated.

I thanked the woman from the bottom of my heart and glanced at my watch. Twelve thirty. The night had just begun. *'Chatzos'*, the precise moment when King David, awoke from his slumber to pour out his heart in supplication and heart rending prayer, to the Master of the Universe, had arrived.

I entered the inner sanctuary and whispered a prayer to R. Shimon and R. Elazar his son, all the while standing in awe of their reverent presence. Men and women, especially women, were standing and trembling, touching their fingertips to their eyes and whispering prayers to R. Shimon and R. Elazar. The holy women's practice, struck at the very chord of my spiritual conscience. They were actually holding conversation with the Holy Tannaim! They were not dead to them. They were very much alive! The inspiration was overwhelming.

On the far left wall, adjacent to R. Shimon's *tzion*, was a long table, both sides full with elderly Sefardic men, engrossed in the recital of the Holy Zohar. I was told, that these men would stay up the whole night, reciting the Zohar in its entirety. What a beautiful sight to behold, indeed. I blessed the Creator for allowing me to live to witness this rare sight of sacrificial devotion.

I had as yet not *davened* maariv, so I positioned myself in a small crevice between the *aron kodesh* and R. Shimon's *tzion*, and began to pray in earnestness. Every word was meticulously enunciated, every thought carefully weighed, as I poured out my heart to Hashem. I can't recall davening such a maariv with so much intensity and fervor, as I had that evening. R. Shimon was not but a mere foot away. I was trembling before G-d. I prayed for my friend, my dear brother's success with regards to his engagement and future. I prayed for myself too. A speedy salvation. My bride to be. I called to my father, of blessed memory, to intercede with R. Shimon at the Heavenly Throne, on my behalf. A half hour maariv. It was one-thirty a.m.

Still somewhat hungry and thirsty, I approached the same good virtuous woman, requesting refreshment, and she more than politely obliged. I thanked her kindly and found a place to sit down among the Zohar scholars. At about a quarter to two, my eyelids began closing and dropping like lead. I had to turn in for the night, but where? I was told that there were rooms upstairs, and that I might check, if there were any still available. I climbed the flight of stone steps in the courtyard, to the balcony level, and began knocking on doors and jarring already open ones. To my disappointment, they were all occupied. Actually, even if they wouldn't have been, I doubt very much if I would have dared to lay my body down on those antiquated, stained mattresses from the stone age. Besides, the rooms were dark and musty; cramped and claustrophobic. More like damp caves.

I descended the flight of steps back to the courtyard and began thinking and wondering how to solve my dilemma. My strength was waning and I needed to lie down, somewhere, anywhere. I exited the courtyard, turned left and proceeded uphill. I returned to the entrance gate and just stood there, contemplating a solution.

"Shalom," someone called to me.

"Shalom," I replied.

"Enjoying yourself?"

"Well I don't know if you could exactly call it that."

"By yourself?"

"Yes, I always travel by myself. I can go where and when I want to. To tour with people is only a hassle, a burdensome weight."

"I'm the same way. I also came up by myself."

"Do you have a place to stay, I mean a bed to sleep in?" I asked.

"That's my problem. I'm looking high and low for an empty room upstairs, but as yet have had no luck in obtaining one. How about you?"

"The same problem. I've been on the road six hours, without proper food and rest, and another two hours here. I need to get some rest and quick. I'm so exhausted."

"You know, if you don't mind to sleep outside of the *tzion* complex, I have an idea for you. There is a school up the hill about a hundred yards from here. See up there?"

"Yes. Yes, now I see it."

"Well, now that it happens to be *bein hazmanim*, between semesters, the school is empty. There are no students present. School starts tomorrow."

"Therefore?"

"I know for a fact that you can obtain foam rubber mattress there."

"And?"

"You place the mattress on the classroom floor, and that's that!"

"By myself?"

"No. No. There are many other people, already fast asleep there right now. Just hope there is a mattress still available. Come, I'll show you the way. Better yet, I'll escort you all the way to the school. I'd like to see what's going on there for myself."

"Thank you very much. You're a big help."

"Don't mention it. What are friends for?"

"You're my friend already?"

"Sure! I sense that we will make very good friends."

"What makes you say that?"

"You came up by yourself and I came up myself. You like to travel alone. So do I. We're made for each other."

"You have a point there. We are definitely similar there."

We walked up the hill together, talking and finding out about each other along the way. When we reached the yeshiva courtyard I remarked, "Everything is so dark and spooky. How come there are no lights on in the building?"

"That's a good question. Maybe, because everybody's sleeping."

We entered the courtyard and proceeded towards the entrance. Once inside the building, we noticed that the only lit light was a fluorescent bulb in the school kitchen. Everything else was pitch black.

"Are you coming up the steps with me, to one of the classrooms?" I asked him.

"No, I don't think so. I'll go back down to the *tzion* complex and try to find a bed there."

"But you said, there weren't any."

"There weren't, but somebody might have left and vacated his bed. I'm going back down."

"But where do I go? Which classrooms are the people using and sleeping in?"

"I don't know. Just go up the steps to the next flight, and open the classroom doors till you find it."

"It's so dark. I don't know if I'll find my way."

"Just follow your hearing sense. If you hear somebody snoring then you know you've found it."

I laughed.

"You'll find it, don't worry," he assured. "Personally, I want to stay near the *tzion*."

"Ok. Listen, thanks alot. I really appreciate it."

"It's nothing at all. Have a good night's sleep."

"Thanks, you too. If you don't find a bed down there, come back here."

"Ok, but how will I find you?"

"Just follow the snoring," I remarked.

Now it was his turn to laugh. With a pat on my back he was off to the *tzion*. I turned towards the stairs. I held on to the bannister tightly and began ascending step by step towards the second floor, where the classrooms were located. My, it was terribly dark. I could see absolutely nothing. Slowly and steadily I reached the top of the stairs, stretched my foot out in front of me and tested the floor for obstructions. Now, where to. My hands instinctively spread out in both directions, searching for something to guide me along. Suddenly and unexpectedly, something touched my fingertips. It was definitely a wall. Now I was getting somewhere. Slowly but surely, I inched my way along the wall and noticed that my eyes were gradually becoming adjusted to the darkness. I could now make out the wall and a few yards of the corridor just ahead. The moonlight was filtering through a window at the end of the corridor and I found it fairly easy to find my way around now.

All I had to do was look for a room with a view. Something nice;

you know with a veranda, champagne in a bucket of ice, and satin sheets on the bed. A thin rubber mat on the floor - what I wouldn't give for one of those now!

I reached the doorway entrance to the first classroom on my right. Empty. Further on down the hall, another classroom. Also empty. Last classroom at the end of the corridor. A huge room with dozens of people on the floor. My eyes scanned and searched for an available rubber mat. There, over by the window, was a vacant one. I stepped gingerly over the snoozing and unassuming fellow roommates toward my destination. Reaching my wonderful bed, I lied down. O, my aching bones. What a relief! My tense muscles began loosening and unwinding. It was about time. Or so I thought.

Thunder. Volcanic eruption. Earthquake. Avalanche. Landslide. No. Not this. An elderly gentleman next to me began snoring uncontrollably. Everybody else was fast asleep. They were dreaming their sweet dreams, whilst I squirmed to try and fall asleep. No use. The philharmonic wind section was busy at work practicing. The percussion division had just joined in. I couldn't take it any more. Then I moved just a bit and let out a soft and gentle sigh and the snorer suddenly exclaimed, "Why are you making so much noise? Can't you be still?!" That did it!

I picked up my mat and left the room. Down the corridor, down the steps and out onto the spacious forecourt veranda. Found a table, placed the mat on it and lied down. The stars above were bright, sparkling and plentiful. What a breathtaking sight. So many stars and so clearly visible at these heights.

I tried to sleep, twisting and turning. On to my right side then onto my left, then on my back. No use. Furthermore, I was afraid of falling off the table. To place the mat on the veranda floor seemed less practical. What if scorpions, spiders or snakes came along. It was also chilly out, and I had no blanket. I was getting cold.

Ok. Here we go again. Off the table. I took the mat in hand and was on my way back into the building, when someone in the dark stopped me.

"Where are you going? What's with the mat?"

"I couldn't sleep inside the building. A guy was snoring uncontrollably. I came down here to the veranda, but it was a bit chilly. I've decided to go back in and find a private quiet corner."

"Wait a minute. There's a group of dormitory buildings just around the back. I'm looking for a place too."

And so, together we hopped up several steps, which brought us to a couple of one story dormitories. Up the entrance steps and inside...

"Who sleeps here?" I inquired.

"I guess the yeshiva students," he replied.

"I see. They're gone now for the semester vacation. There are plenty of empty beds. Still we have no permission to use them. Besides, you might get woken up in the middle of the night by the guy who's bed you're sleeping in! That wouldn't be too nice would it. I mean, they could come back late tonight, since tomorrow is the start of the new semester."

We both concluded that our sleeping quarters for the night would have to be somewhere else. I went back inside the yeshiva building. Up the steps, to the same corridor, but this time I entered an empty classroom, placed my mat on the floor, lied down on it and tried to fall asleep. Four in the morning. I couldn't fall asleep. I was a bit apprehensive to be alone and in the dark. What if somebody opened the door and decided to rob me. He could pull it off without a hitch. And hurt me too. Visions of a prowler standing menacingly above me, began haunting my thoughts.

These thoughts circuited my mind, until sleep finally took over and my totally exhausted and drained body, gave in to the sweet realm of relaxation. As I had no blanket to keep me warm, my sleep did not last very long and at about five thirty I awoke. An hour and a half of sleep. Not too bad. Better than nothing. I got up, went downstairs to the kitchen, washed my hands, and took a drink of water. Then I proceeded downhill towards the *tzion* for shacharis.

The first *minyan* began at six thirty, and was over at seven thirty. I remembered that there was a small restaurant, right outside the courtyard. I approached the quaint little kiosk-restaurant, but was disappointed to find it closed.

"Good morning!" someone behind me exclaimed. I turned around. It was my friend.

"Good morning," I said. "And how are you today?"

"Don't ask. I was up a whole night. Couldn't find a bed."

"Well, what do you think I went through last night! In the darkness of night, I groped through classrooms, looking for an available mat.

Then a guy started snoring like a locomotive, and I went outside and tried to fall asleep on a table."

"What?!"

"It was too risky. I was afraid I would roll off. On the floor, I would be an excellent meal for a snake. Besides it was too chilly and I didn't have a blanket to cover me."

"So what did you do then?"

"I took the mat, went back into the building, and fell asleep in an empty classroom."

"What time was that?"

"About four."

"What time did you wake up?"

"About five-thirty."

"Not bad. At least you got more than an hour's sleep. That's more than I got," he complained.

"You must be knocked out."

"That's not the word for it."

"So what are you going to do now?"

"I'm starving for breakfast."

"Me too. I'm waiting for the kiosk to open."

"It's supposed to open about eight thirty."

"What are you doing after breakfast?" I asked.

"Oh, I don't know yet. Maybe, I'll go to Teverya, to R. Meir Baal Haness, and to the Rambam. Maybe, if I have time, I'll go to R. Akiva too. After that, I'd like to go to Kiryat Shemoneh and Metullah. What are your plans?"

"Well, I would like very much to go to Amukah. I'm..."

"Oh, I see."

"Have you ever been to Amukah?" I asked.

"Yes, now that you mention it, I have."

"Do you know how I can get there?"

"By yourself? Are you serious?"

"Why can't I go by myself?"

"Nobody goes by themselves."

"Why not?"

"Why not? Because it's dangerous."

"I'm going by day. What could be dangerous about that?"

"It's not the time of day that matters, it's the place."

"What do you mean? Where is it?"

"It's in a deep valley in a hidden vast forest somewhere between Tzefas and Hatzor. Nobody goes by themselves."

"Well, then how do people get there?"

"By taxi."

"Well, I suppose I could get a few guys together to share a taxi. Do you want to go?"

"To tell you the truth, no. I've been there already. I'd like to go, where I've never been before. I like new things. I'm adventurous. But you go on ahead. I'm sure you'll find people who'll join you in renting a taxi."

Chapter Three

Attempt to Amukah

"Perhaps I'll start looking for a taxi and prospective travelers right now," I remarked, scanning the parking lot.
"That's a good idea. Until breakfast anyhow I'll help you along."
"Thanks."
As we turned round, a taxi approached and stopped a few yards distance. My friend and I approached and inquired of the driver, whether he would be interested in going to Amukah. "No," he flatly declared. Next. Another taxi approached. He also declined.
We kept on asking, but kept on getting no for an answer.
"There must be a way to get there, without a taxi. I just know that there has to exist a way for an individual to get there."
"There isn't, believe me," he said. "As far as I know, everyone of my friends has traveled there either by taxi or mini bus."
"But you said, it was situated between Tzefas and Hatzor. I don't see why I couldn't take a bus to either Tzefas or Hatzor, and hike from there."
"Are you serious? Would you walk through the forest by yourself?"
"Why not, if I had the proper directions."
"No, no. That's much too dangerous. You would get lost. Besides, there are wild animals up there."
"But I must get there. I just must. The main purpose of my trip is getting to Amukah!"
"Don't worry. You'll get there. Just keep at it. You'll find the people, and the driver to take you there. Perseverance."
We heard the sudden noise of a wooden slat window being opened behind us. Breakfast was served.
The smell of scrambled eggs and toast filled the morning air. We sat down at a cute little table, one of only three in the whole place, and had breakfast.

"By the way, what's your name?" my new found friend inquired.
"Mutty. What's yours?"
"Yoily."

I guess independent travellers were likewise very independent about a distinct willingness to keep their names to themselves. We respected each other now without reservation and so we volunteered our top secrets to one another with a sense of mutual understanding and trust.

Breakfast over, we *bentched* and went back outside to resume our task of looking for candidates and a taxi to Amukah. I glanced at my watch. It was already nine-thirty. Time was moving on.

Yoily and I split up, in the hope of canvassing people for my excursion. At about ten o'clock we met back at the courtyard entrance gate with still no luck.

"Yoily, it's no use. It's already ten o'clock and I'm still here."
"So am I."
"Sorry. I'd really like to thank you for helping me. I've taken up already too much of your precious time. You go on to Teverya. I'll take care of myself. Don't worry, I'll get to Amukah even if I have to go through fire and water. You know our kind. We're independent."
"I understand exactly what you mean. I'm sure you'll get there and *daven* well for your *zivug*, and will be able to tell me good news very soon."
"Amen."
"Alright. I'm going to get ready. So I'll say to you *l'hitraot*."
"I'll see you here tonight, ok?"
"About what time?"
"Mincha or maariv time."
"Very good. Then we'll work together on finding a place to sleep tonight. I don't think I can go on like this. If I don't find a bed, then I'll just have to cut my trip short, and hitch a ride back to my school in Kiryat Sanz, Natanya."
"That would be a shame," I remarked.
"You bet it would. I really want to stay, another day."
"Or more."
"Ok, it's getting late. Have to get a move on. The bus stop is down the road, on the main highway. The bus runs every half hour. It's ten twenty. If I leave right now, I could still make the ten-thirty bus."
"Don't waste a second. Get a move on."
"Bye, and good luck.

"Thanks, you too."

And he was off. I turned to enter the courtyard and suddenly...

"Mutty, Mutty!"

I turned round, and noticed Yoily, waiving at me, beckoning me to come quick. I rushed over to him, inquiring what had happened.

"This man has a taxi. He says, he's going to Amukah."

"Wonderful!" I exclaimed.

"He has room for one more passenger. It's a seven passenger Mercedes taxi. He already has six, and is looking for one more."

"Oh, that's great. Yoily, thanks alot. But you have to rush or you'll miss the bus!"

"Yes, I almost forgot! Bye!"

"Bye, and thanks alot again. See you tonight!"

"Looking forward to it," and he was off and running. It was Ten twenty-three. I hoped that he'd make it. He was such a wonderful person.

I stood glued to the taxi, waiting patiently for the original passengers to return from their visit to the *tzion*. Twenty minutes later, four of the passengers returned. I approached one of them and informed him, that I would be the seventh passenger. He was pretty upset with my statement, and immediately began having a heated discussion with the taxi driver. I understood every word...

"What do you mean by squashing another guy in? We rented the taxi for six, not seven. We made a set price with you."

"Listen, there's room for seven! It's a seven passenger car!"

"But we rented the whole taxi, and we explicitly told you, only for six. Not more!"

"Don't be such a miser."

"If you insist upon taking a seventh passenger, then we'll just leave you, and you won't get paid a *grush*."

"Are you threatening me?"

"No, just the facts. Get them clear and straight."

"You're not the boss, anyway. I'm waiting for the one who rented the taxi from me. What he says, I'll listen to, not you."

"Suit yourself."

Ten minutes later the remaining two passengers arrived. The driver began speaking with one of them. Then the fellow who was against the whole idea of a seventh passenger joined in. I was standing right there, but they thought I didn't understand.

"It's ok with me," said the one who rented the taxi. "But he has to take a share in the expense."

"What do you mean," the taxi driver retorted. "He has to pay extra!"

"Oh , no. You want to squash in a seventh passenger and he should add to your pocket? If he shares our expense, then I'll agree, if not, forget it."

"You know what, forget it," the driver declared.

I immediately interjected.

"I'll pay my price, and take a share in the taxi expense. How about that?"

The heated fellow interjected, "No, I don't want it. We agreed on six passengers and no more, and that's final."

The fine decent fellow, turned to me, and with a sympathetic expression on his face, said, "I hope you'll understand. I'm sorry."

"It's ok. I understand."

"Don't be angry."

"I'm not. It's just that my hopes were so high and then all of a sudden they dropped."

"You'll get there, don't worry. There'll be other taxis. The day has just begun."

"Thanks for the encouragement," I said, as I slowly backed away.

They all packed into the taxi, as I drew a deep sigh of frustration, and turned painfully to watch it pull away without me. That's the breaks. The taxi was now completely out of view. I turned and headed towards the courtyard entrance. Sad and dejected, my head bent low, I drooped and drew a deep sigh, as I changed direction and entered the quaint coffee shop kiosk where I had breakfast earlier.

"You. Yes you! You were looking for a ride to Amukah?" someone called out.

"Yes," I replied. "Yes, indeed! Do you know of a ride?"

"There is a woman here with a taxi, who wants to get to Amukah. She says she has place for two. Ask the driver if he has place for you."

I thanked him excitedly. I spotted the taxi immediately. As I approached, I noticed several people standing near the driver and they were requesting a spot to Amukah. The driver assured me that there was one more available seat for me, and that he would be leaving momentarily with the woman. She was still praying at the *tzion* and he would await her arrival any moment. I thanked him kindly and waited patiently by the car. Five minutes later she arrived.

"I can tell you the directions to Amukah, if you agree to allow my friend here to come along with me," a person remarked to the woman.

The driver responded pointing to me, "But this fellow here — I've already promised him the remaining seat."

He replied, "But you don't know the way to Amukah. You need me to show you the way, and I'm not going without my friend here."

The driver asked the woman what to do. She asked me if I knew the way. I said I didn't. She explained gently that she had no other choice but to give in to his demands. I nodded that I understood. She said she was very sorry.

I watched them get into the taxi and pull away. I would have to start all over again.

This Amukah was eluding me but why? Then I remembered my eldest brothers' words to me on that sorrowful night when the *'Shiva'* candle which had been lit in my father's memory went out for the second time.

"You know," he said to me, "I've given it a bit of thought. I think the light keeps going out because it possesses *kedushah*. The more holy a thing the more Satan tries to obstruct it. It's a test from heaven. We must never give up. I'll just re-light it."

After he had said those words the light stayed lit for the remainder of the *'Shiva'* days. It was a perfect analogy to my present situation. My desire to reach Amukah was a holy undertaking. Satan wasn't too pleased with that and was therefore trying to discourage me from attempting the trip. Good. Excellent. I would not give in. If not today, then tomorrow. But I would get there. Yes, *B'ezras Hashem*, I would pray at R. Yonoson's side. Satan would have to get his armor oiled if he decided to continue sparring with me. The fact that getting to Amukah was going to be a difficult task to achieve made it that more interesting to pursue.

I glanced at my watch. It was almost eleven o'clock. The day was half gone. I figured that by the time I could organize concrete arrangements for the trip, it would be too late to set out. I decided to spend the rest of the day in and around Meiron. Tomorrow, I would try again. If need be, I would set out by bus and foot.

Now to see Meiron and its environs, but first lunch. I had a tuna fish sandwich in pita bread and a glass of orange juice. A piece of cake for desert and I was ready to go.

Chapter Four

Kissei Eliyahu

I remembered seeing a sign near the *tzion* courtyard entrance, with a list of *mekomos hakedoshim* on it in the immediate vicinity to visit.

I approached the large green sign, and took note of the interesting places to see: *"Hillel v'talmidov," "Shammai v'kaloso,"* and *"Kissei Eliyahu."* What exactly was K*issei Eliyahu*? Didn't my younger brother once show me a picture of himself standing on top of an enormous rock, which he indicated was *Kissei Eliyahu*? Yes, it was coming back to me now. *Kissei Eliyahu*, was a large rock outcrop, situated in the middle of a forest slope on a mountain side near *Har Meiron*. It is said that from the top of this very stone, *Eliyahu Hanavi* will announce "the good news." From this very spot, he is destined to announce the coming of the Messiah.

My younger brother related how difficult it was trying to climb the rock, as its sides were smooth and straight all the way to the top. His friends helped him all the way up, and then took his picture.

Kissei Eliyahu. Interesting. Mystical. Holy. Could I perhaps see it from here? I approached a young fellow, and inquired, "I see the sign here says *Kissei Eliyahu*, with an arrow pointing towards the right. Is that correct?"

"Actually, *Kissei Eliyahu* is the last *makom kadosh* on the trail. First, the path approaches Hillel and his *talmidim*, and then it curves and weaves by *Shammai v'kaloso*. After that, you just have to follow your sense of direction by keeping your eyes fixed on that stone constantly. If you lose sight of it for even one moment, you can get lost."

"Can you direct me?"

"Let me show you."

We went up the side stone steps to the *tzion* balcony and he pointed with his finger.

"Do you see it, over there?"

"Where?"

"Over there. No, not the second mountain. The uphill slope of the third mountain three quarters of the way up."

"One second, I'm scanning. Yes, yes, now I see it."

"Of course, it's the only stone formation on the whole mountain side. Everything else is covered with shrubs, bushes and trees."

"Then I shouldn't have any problem keeping it in my sight."

"Well not exactly. You see, from our vantage point, the stone is clearly visible. But when you get to the actual slope, your angle of vision towards the stone will become disturbed. You'll be looking upwards at a seventy-five degree angle, with bushes and trees in the way, attributing to a severe obstruction of vision. You might get confused, when you lose sight of it for a moment and may find yourself climbing upwards still, but in the wrong direction. I know people who lost it half way up and found themselves on a longer sojourn than expected."

"What do you suggest I do?"

"Well, I'll suggest to you what not to do. Don't go alone."

"It's not that dangerous, I should think."

"Do you know how far away that stone is from here?"

"About half a mile."

"Half a mile?!"

"More?"

"More?! *Kissei Eliyahu* is more than three miles away!"

"It doesn't look that distant."

"It looks close, but believe me it's not. I know. First you have to take the trail past *Hillel v'talmidov*. Then the path slopes down into the deep valley and crosses over the stream called Mayyan Meggido. Then it continues past *sabra* bushes, and curves left and begins its steep upward climb towards *Shammai v'kaloso*. That alone will take you over an hour."

"You mean going down into the valley and up the second mountain?"

"Yes. It's not as easy as it looks."

"Then, from *Shammai v'kaloso*, how much more to go?"

"About a half hour more."

"That's an hour and a half to *Kissei Eliyahu*."

"If you don't stop to rest."

"Round trip, with resting, would be around three, three and a half hours."

"That's right."

I glanced at my watch. It was twelve o'clock. If I set out now, I'd be back at three, three-thirty.

"I suggest you go right away. Once it starts getting dark, it can become pretty hazardous out there. You could lose your whole sense of direction, *chas v'shalom*."

"Yes, you're definitely right."

"Come down the steps with me. I'll start you on the path."

We went down the steps, passed the green sign, and he began...

"You see over there; go down those steps and continue straight ahead for about a hundred yards. The cave containing *Hillel v'talmidov* will be over to your right. You'll see the sign. To continue on your way after that, follow the sign that points towards the valley of Mayyan Meggido. It's pretty steep, so take it slow down. Once you get to the bottom of the valley, cross over the tiny stream, using the wide wooden plank. When you have crossed the stream, you will notice a dense thicket of sabra bushes to your right. Continue on straight ahead until a path seems to suddenly appear. The path will begin ascending the second mountain; curving left, as it climbs steeply upwards. It will then curve to the right and upwards, straight away. When the path has leveled off, you will see the *tzion* of *Shammai v'kalaso* before you."

"What does it look like?"

"To describe it, I would say it resembles a small stone hut with smooth, wind-polished granite blocks, placed one on top of another, forming a little dwelling habitat for Shammai and his daughter-in-law."

"Interesting."

"From there, you should be able to see *Kissei Eliyahu* very clearly. Just follow your nose and keep it in sight as you climb and remember, don't lose sight of it even for a second. Try to stay clear of the dense brush. If you must enter the brush, make sure your eyes stay glued to the stone. You want to retain the proper direction at all times."

"Very important to know. Thanks."

"Well you'd better get a move on. It's getting late."

"Yes, I'm going right now. Thank you very much for your time and effort, and above all your splendid and patient manner of explaining everything in vivid detail. I am much obliged to your kind assistance."

"Don't mention it. You just get back here safe and sound."

"*B'ezras Hashem*. Thank you again."

"*Hatzlacha*."

And I was off. I proceeded down the steps, and on the pathway towards *Hillel v'talmidov*. Several minutes later, a bright red sign with white letters appeared. It said '*Hillel v'talmidov*' and had an arrow pointing towards a cave entrance several yards to its right.

Once inside the cave, I noticed the many lit candles which illuminated the dark recesses and crypts of the spacious cavern. Hillel, prince of Israel, a direct descendant of King David, and his illustrious disciples graced this seemingly void, dark and desolate cave with their sacred presence. Was I actually here? Or was I dreaming that I was standing before these holy Tannaim. I had spent many years studying about Hillel and his disciples, their rulings in Torah Law, their attitudes in life and above all their self-sacrifice and devotion to *avodas Hashem m'ahava*, serving G-d from love.

But now, for the first time in my life, this dream of coming close to these angels, had materialized. A tingling sensation travelled up and down my spine, as my lips offered an emotional prayer, imploring these great saints to intercede upon Israel's behalf, in granting them their needs and salvations, my *zivug* included in the bundle of requests.

I picked up two candles from the cave floor and lit one in memory of the holy Mishnah sages present and the other in the cherished memory of my dear, beloved father, *olov hashalom*. Then I stood for a moment thinking, contemplating, absorbing, comprehending, taking it all in. These were miracle workers. Men of another realm in time. Spiritual super-beings. Individuals who had mastered absolute control over their inclinations and desires. Eagles of sanctity, soaring to heights way above the clouds, and far beyond the stars. To be in the presence of such supernatural beings was indeed a special merit and privilege, and I thanked Hashem Yisborach for granting me the opportunity to savor every moment of it. More than two thousand years of history was staring me in the eye, strengthening the ties between ancestor and descendant, fortifying the unshakable faith in G-d, and solidifying an inherent deep trust in Him. The Talmud existed. The Tannaim existed. The never ending chain from the Holy Patriarchs has continued uninterrupted till the present generation, and will continue, by being strengthened through Torah-enriched links, galvanized by a spiritual fire burning within the innermost chamber of Israel's heart.

Pure holy water, in the form of joyous tears have streamed down the faces of G-d's children, generation after generation, nourishing the blossoms of faith and trust, enriching the soil with an indestructible belief in the coming of Moshiach and the final glorious redemption.

A testimony of truth, a witness to the authenticity of G-d and His Torah Law, was what this cavern actually symbolized. A signification of *nitzchius*, 'infiniteness,' and a landmark testifying to the children of Israel as G-d's chosen people.

Strange as it may seem, this lifeless cave was very much alive, imbued with two thousand years of faith, trust, hope and truth, in effect, a beacon in the darkness of night, directing those who have sincerely searched for G-d over the generations in an never ending quest, to discover the supreme goodness, that is, G-d.

And here I was, fortunate and privileged to be standing and witnessing a panorama of vivid history spanning well over two millennium. I never dreamed that one day I'd actually find myself standing in the presence of Hillel the elder. What's more, Shammai, Hillel's counterpart, was not too far away, a thought which sent more chills up and down my spine. I would set out momentarily. It was getting late.

I concluded my visit with a prayer for *Techiyas HaMeisim, b'meherah*, and politely excused myself from their holy presence, as I exited the cave into the afternoon sun. It would be best to get a move on.

I scanned the immediate area, and spotted a sign which read, "*Mayyan Meggido - Shammai v'kalaso.*" Mayyan Meggido was the trickling spring at the bottom of the valley. I would have to cross it, to reach *Shammai v'kalaso*. I followed the direction of the arrow, till it led me to another sign and a pathway near it leading down towards the valley floor.

"Careful now. Don't rush down that path. It looks and seems easier then it actually is," someone called to me.

I turned to notice a group of hiking youngsters approaching. I thanked them wholeheartedly for the thoughtful cautious warning, and began the descent. I soon found out that they were actually right. The steep terrain coupled with the hidden jagged rocks and lush roots, slowed my progress to a snail's pace.

Slowly but surely, I finally reached the valley floor. Now to cross the spring. Ah yes. There, not more than a couple of yards away, was the wooden board, the plank I was told about. Reaching it, I placed one foot upon it to test the board for strength and sturdiness. It seemed ok so I placed the other foot on and began the crossing. Steady now. "Keep your balance," I kept on telling myself. Twenty seconds later, I was on the other side. Now where to. The sabra bushes. Yes, there they were towards the right. I was to continue on past them, in the direction of the second mountain, which would lead me to an ascending dirt road.

Suddenly, as if out of nowhere, two youngsters appeared from the sabra bushes.

"Shalom."

"Shalom to you and what are you doing down here by yourselves? Isn't it rather dangerous? You could get lost."

"We come down here practically every day. We live up the mountain not far from R. Shimon's *tzion*. Now's the season for picking ripe sabras. You have to be very careful when you pick them. They have tiny prickly needles which sting, if you don't know how to go about it. And what are you doing down here."

"I'm on my way to *Shammai v'kalaso*, and then on to *Kissei Eliyahu*. By the way, am I in the right direction?"

"Yes. Just continue straight ahead, till you see a path. Stay on that path till you come to a fork in the road. Turn to your left. The path will widen into a dirt road, and will begin ascending this mountain."

"If I keep on going straight, I'll find myself on the path?"

"Yes."

"It must be around the back of the mountain towards the left."

"Yes, you have to curve to the left, you'll see it when you get closer."

"Thanks alot boys. *Hatzlacha* in your sabra picking."

"We've already picked half of them. Look at our baskets." They were full to the brim.

"Let me try and pick one."

"Careful. You have to know how to do it, without getting stung."

"Don't worry, I'm an expert."

I approached one of the bushes and proceeded to pick a sabra fruit...

"Ouch! That hurts!"

"See, we told you so. You have to wear gloves or protect your fingers with aluminum foil or paper. If you're really an expert you can do it with your bare hands. Watch."

And they both picked the sabras with their bare hands with amazing ease. It was definitely a skill.

"I must admit, it looks easy. I'll have to learn how to do it one day. For now I best get a move on. Thanks for the directions."

"You're welcome."

"Shalom."

"Shalom."

And I was on my way. A little while later the aforementioned path suddenly appeared. A hundred yards more and I approached the fork in the road. I turned to my left and noticed that the path widened gradually as it ascended the mountain side. Upwards, I trudged, climbing the path's steep incline, pausing intermittently to rest and catch my breath. Half way up the slope the path curved sharply to the right, just as the fellow said it would. Then it continued straight away but very steep in the going. I had to stop several times to retain my store of energy.

At about one o'clock the path suddenly leveled off, and I found myself standing before a small clearing. And there it was! In the middle of the clearing stood the small stone hut! Smooth granite blocks, placed neatly one on another, forming a miniature stone villa, square in shape.

I approached the sacred *tzion* slowly and cautiously. I stood with awe and reverence as my fingers gently caressed the wind polished stones. They were enormous in size. Who had erected this edifice? How long ago was it put up? Could these stones possibly date back to the Holy Temple era? An astounding chapter in history and an additional segment of my holy ancestry, to marvel and wonder at.

I walked around the structure and noticed a small opening in the wall two feet square in size, situated about four feet above the ground. It seemed to lead into the interior of the *tzion*. I stuck my head in and observed two rectangular stone slabs, side by side, and quickly realized that underneath them lay the holy beings of *Shammai v'kaloso*. How terribly and frighteningly holy was this place! Shammai, Hillel's master counterpart in all aspects of Torah law, was at eternal rest before me, his holy daughter-in-law at his side.

The opening in the stone wall was just big enough for a person to crawl through. I pulled myself up and in, elbow on elbow, and slowly inched my way into the interior. After an extended effort, I lay my tired body down upon Shammai's stone. There was not an inch to move in either direction.

Tears swelled up in my eyes. "Collect my tears and bring them before the Heavenly Throne. The joy of my dearest friend yearns to dispel the sorrow of my heart. Yet the pain becomes more unbearable with each passing day. I feel incomplete. Something is missing."

And for a short moment, I lay still, absorbing the reality of where I was. One could not get any closer to Shammai. It was all like a fairy tale dream. Shammai, Hillel's equal in Torah wisdom!

My teardrops had collected within the etchings of the stone and became absorbed into the letter's of Shammai's name. A feeling of sublime relief permeated my being as I felt a heavy weight being lifted off my chest. An inner feeling sensed that my prayer had already ascended to heaven and had been accepted. "And please, if my dearest friend has found his true zivug, then he should experience only happiness and joy with her. May they have a life of success and merit to behold a *bayis ne'eman b'yisroel*. However if she is not his preordained *zivug*, then please, please save him from peril. You Hashem, You alone know everything hidden. Protect him for he is my brother."

The depths of my heart had spoken. I sensed that all would be well. Slowly and cautiously, elbow to elbow I crawled backwards out of the *tzion*. The fresh open air entered my lungs and I breathed deeply. My eyes squinted as they accustomed themselves to the sudden burst of sunlight.

As I turned to take leave of the Holy *tzion*, my eyes caught sight of something very interesting. There, in a hidden alcove, not twenty yards behind the *tzion*, was what seemed to be a temple ruin: marble pillars, stone steps; in effect, the remains of what looked to be *Bais Shammai*! Could it possibly actually be The House where Shammai expounded his interpretations on the Torah Law? I approached the ruin, and marveled at the majestic marble pillars crowned by magnificent capitals; a work of artistic craftsmanship which definitely dated back to the Holy Temple era. I sat down on a stone step and began contemplating the voices, the prayers, the heated Torah debates that must have resounded within these confines more than two thousand years ago. It was like going back in time.

I stood up and walked over to the opposite end of the ancient ruin, and was suddenly taken aback by a magnificent view, a breathtaking landscape of luscious green mountains for as far as the eye could see. "How great are Your works O Hashem!" I stood there for a couple of moments taking in the beautiful scenery, and then turned to leave as I had felt that I should be getting a move on. I glanced at my watch. It was one-twenty. I ascended the four enormous stone steps, and exited the temple ruins. Now to *Kissei Eliyahu*.

I scanned the slope up ahead, and there – there it was. About three quarters of the way up the mountain side, in the midst of dense brush and foliage. I had to remember to keep my eyes fixed on that location, at all times. Doing so, I proceeded past *Shammai v'kalaso*, touching the *tzion* and murmuring a prayer as I passed by, and continued on towards the foot of the slope. The clearing had turned to dense brush and thorns as I began the uphill trudge.

There seemed to be somewhat of a path a couple of yards up the slope so I decided to follow it, in the hope that it would eventually lead me to the Holy Stone. Upwards I climbed, panting and sweating under the hot sun, my eyes not moving from the stone for even a second.

Then, the path suddenly disappeared into the dense brush. I surmised that since so few travelers took the difficult trek to *Kissei Eliyahu*, dense foliage proliferated the entire area around the stone with the passage of time.

As I had no pathway to guide me now, the importance of keeping my eyes fixed on the sacred stone became more imperative. The going starting becoming rough. There was practically no where to get a footing. I began hopping and jumping between the thorns and dense thistles. The thorns really scratched. The higher I got the more dense the brush became. It was getting more and more difficult to proceed.

I glanced upwards remembering to keep my eye on the stone, but to my disbelief it was gone! Vanished! I knew it. I had been so preoccupied with avoiding the sharp thorns, that I had completely forgotten about keeping tabs on the stone. Where did it go? It was right over there just a couple of seconds ago! That fellow warned me, "Don't lose sight of it, even for one moment." Well, there was nothing for me to do now but to improvise by utilizing my intuition and sense of direction.

I continued the ascent, adjusting the direction of my movements, accordingly. I figured, the higher I'd get, the more chance I'd have of bringing it into view again. But I was wrong. The higher I got, the taller the brush became, thus complicating the situation and predicament even further.

My forehead was dripping beads of sweat, as I shot a quick glance at my wristwatch. It was almost two o'clock! I had already spent more than a half hour climbing the slope, yet there was no sight of the stone. "Never give up," I told myself. "Keep on going and you'll get there."

And so, I trudged on, hopping and jumping through the thicket, trying to avoid the sharp thorns and thistles.

At about two-fifteen I experienced a miracle. The stone miraculously appeared! It was to my right about a hundred yards distant. I had gone completely off course and would have passed and missed it entirely, if it weren't for me stubbing my toe on a jagged rock. The sudden mishap caused me to drop to my knees, and that's when I saw it. It looked much different from this angle.

I worked my way across to about ten yards from the sacred stone. A somewhat peculiar sight, considering its location and size. The only rock formation on the entire mountain side. Everything else was just dense brush. The fact that it was the only stone for miles around seemed to indicate that it indeed possessed a mysterious hidden mystical significance. I came up to it and placed my hands upon its smooth sides, my eyes staring towards the summit. It was about twelve feet high and approximately four feet square in width.

To think that Eliyahu would one day announce the Messiah's arrival from the top of this very stone! It sent chills up and down my spine.

I surveyed the walls of the rock and determined that I could not possibly scale it to the top without the help of a companion. I therefore prayed, "Hashem, you know how much I want to stand upon the summit, upon the spot where Eliyahu, your faithful servant, will one day stand and proclaim the imminent arrival of David's son, but unfortunately I cannot accomplish this alone. Please, dear G-d, may it be considered in Your eyes, as if I had stood upon the summit of this holy stone, and offered a prayer from that sacred spot."

I kissed the stone, and embraced it lovingly. I whispered a silent fervent prayer and turned to depart. It was two-twenty.

I scanned the far off distant area and spotted the stone hut of *Shammai v'kalaso* on the mountain slope down below. I would use the *tzion* as a landmark to assist and guide me in my return trip. The going now would be much easier since it would be downhill most of the way.

About twenty-five minutes later, I approached *Shammai v'kalaso* and touched its smooth stones once again. I murmured a prayer, and was on my way. The temple ruin twenty yards off caught my attention at the last moment, and I had an inner prodding to visit it too before I moved on, so I approached one of its marble pillars, placed a hand on it, offered a silent prayer, and continued my trek home.

I proceeded down the dirt road, which eventually curved towards the left, and continued straight down to the foot of the mountain. There, I turned right and walked straight away until I reached the sabra bushes. It was a little after four, when I decided to try my luck at picking another sabra..."Ouch!"

I moved on, holding my bruised finger delicately in my other hand. I came to the trickling stream and crossed the wooden plank to the other side. Once safely across, I searched for the pathway that would lead me up the mountain slope, to the original path which would take me back to the Rashbi. Locating it, I scampered up the trail with revitalized strength, in spite of my body's exhausted condition.

Half way up the slope, my legs and lungs begged for a rest. Who was I kidding? My physical endurance had already been pushed to the limit. I sat my weary body down upon a rock and rested a bit. Several minutes later, I stood up and continued on my way. The upward climb slackened to a snail's pace. The energy reserve tank was registering 'empty.'

I glanced upwards and was relieved to notice that I was not more than twenty yards from the aforementioned path. Steadily I climbed, experiencing a sudden surge of energy as I quickened my pace to a brisk tempo in the intent of getting it over with. Before I knew it, I found myself standing on the path not ten yards from the sign which read *'Hillel v'talmidov.'* I drew a deep sigh of relief and blessed Hashem for returning me safe and sound.

I walked the ten yards to the cave and entered. I whispered a silent prayer, lit a candle and continued on the final leg of my return trek. At about three o'clock, I finally stood at the courtyard entrance to the Rashbi. I was home. An exhausting three hours.

I proceeded to the kiosk, purchased a bottle of soda water and downed it in fifteen seconds flat. I purchased another one and finished it almost as fast. The cool, refreshing liquid revived me a bit. I sat down and rested upon a stone bench trying to relax my aching bones.

Chapter Five

A Good Night's Sleep

"Well Hello!"

I spun around.

"Yoily, you're back!"

"Yes, I'm back. I went to Tzefas. I didn't quite make it to Teverya, but what about you? I thought you would have been in Amukah by now."

I told him briefly of my disappointments and about my tour of Meiron and its environs. We ate a little meal at the quaint kiosk and talked a bit.

"What about a place to stay for tonight? Think we'll find a place around here to sleep," I asked Yoily.

"Sure hope so. If not, then we'll both have to go back home."

"Well, Yoily, I'm beat and I've got a terrible headache. I'm going to see if I can find a place to lie down. After that, I think I'll go to Tzefas for mincha and maariv. I'll meet you back here in the evening, ok?"

"Fine with me. I think I'm going to hitch to Teverya now, to the *mekomos hakedoshim*. I'll be back at night. See you then."

"*Kol tuv*," and we parted.

The two small bottles of soda water and miniscule amount of food could not have been expected to quell my acute dizziness from lack of sleep and I knew that I'd better lie down soon. My aching and tired head weighed like lead.

The school up the hill came to mind. Perhaps I could catch a quick nap there, if I could find a mat and provided the boys hadn't returned from their semester recess yet, which would mean the classrooms were still empty and available.

I walked uphill a hundred yards or so, mustering whatever strength I had left. Once inside the school building, I was surprised to notice how different everything looked by the light of day. I recalled how, just the other night, I had groped in the darkness, not knowing where I was going.

I ascended the flight of stairs to the classrooms level, but was very disappointed to find that the classroom which had been full of mats the night before was now occupied with neatly arranged rows of school desks and chairs.

"There must be a classroom with a remaining mat in it, there just has to be," I said to myself reassuringly.

Sure enough, a classroom at the end of the hall did contain a single mat although some desks and chairs were already present. I felt gratitude to the *Ribono Shel Olam*.

I positioned the mat in the corner of the room behind a desk and chair in order to be out of the way. I would have my privacy which would let me rest and unwind. I laid my weary body down on the rubber mat and exhaled, stretching my aching leg muscles and tired bones. Now to catch a nap. I was so overtired and so over-wound that sleep evaded me. It just would not come. I was too tense and rigid. After all, I had been actively mobile since the previous afternoon and had not gotten the opportunity to rejuvenate my faculties.

Suddenly, the classroom door opened and several pairs of feet entered. Voices and conversation. Several minutes later they were gone. Moments later, a single pair of feet entered, shlepped around and left. Then it happened again. It was no use. Even if I would have happened to be in the proper physical and mental condition to fall asleep, still, the constant disturbance would have obstructed any possible attempt to achieve it. It was an agonizing feeling of utter frustration.

I glanced at my watch. About ten to five. At least I had benefited from a sixty minute rest. I had to content myself with this short repose. It was better than nothing.

As I rose, I felt the immediate benefits derived from the duration of my relaxation. My head wasn't spinning or heavy anymore. I could continue on, till the night of course, but no more. I would have to call it quits and travel home if I could not obtain a place of lodging for the night, a saddening thought which left a bitter taste in my mouth, as in that unfortunate event, I would have no other choice but to forgo and give up all hope of reaching Amukah! I pushed that unappealing thought out of my mind and decided that my determination would overpower and subdue Satan's doubts as to my fortitude and will.

Five o'clock. Time for Tzefas. I stretched my arms and neck muscles and exhaled. I would *daven* earnestly and felt confident that Hashem Yisborach would direct my friend and I to a comfortable place of lodging for the night.

I went down the mountain towards the Rashbi courtyard but an interesting bright red sign at the road side caught the attention of my eye. It said "R. Yochanan HaSandler" with an arrow pointing in the direction of a narrow asphalt road towards the right.

I inquired of a passerby as to how far down the road I'd have to go to reach the *tzion* and he replied that it would be no more than five minutes. I had plenty of time for mincha in Tzefas so I decided to visit the holy *tzion*.

Several yards down the path, I stopped and stood transfixed with awe as I witnessed a crowd of people standing around what seemed to be a lamb, bleating at the hands of a *shochet*. A few seconds later and the bleating stopped. The ritual handed down from generation to generation was still alive and vibrant. G-d's Law to Israel. "Look R. Shimon! Behold your children walk in G-d's way!" I exclaimed, standing on the hilltop overlooking the *mekom hashechita*. "A chosen people who have not strayed from Heaven's Law. Have mercy upon them and intercede upon their behalf, before the Heavenly Celestial Throne!"

As I continued towards R. Yochanan HaSandler I kept my eyes upon the shochet and observed his step by step systematical method in conjunction with his activities. He handled the situation with the greatest of ease.

About two hundred yards down the road, the *tzion* came into view. I blessed Hashem for allowing my eyes to benefit from such a holy sight as this. I approached the sacred resting place of R. Yochanan HaSandler, 'the shoe maker' ('cobbler') and proclaimed, "A shoe mender! - Indeed!" As Hillel chopped wood and R. Eliezer carried water jugs. "Fortunate are you R. Yochanan, for you were not ashamed to assume the honorable responsibility of *derech eretz*!"

I kissed the stone and whispered a prayer. I took leave of the *tzion*, by stepping three steps backwards, and bid farewell to the Holy Tanna.

Twenty minutes later, I was standing on the main road to Tzefas. The bus arrived and I hopped on. Eight kilometers down the road, the bus pulled into the *Tachana Merkazit* of Tzefas. I got off, and walked to the Ari Shul, where mincha and maariv were *davened*. Afterwards I had supper at the quaint Eshel Restaurant, off Rechov Yerushalayim.

At about nine o'clock, I found myself standing on the road at the exit of the town, just opposite the Central Bus Station. That's where everyone hitches to Meiron. I figured that by now there would be much more room in Meiron, owing to probable reasoning that many of its visitors would have left her by tonight.

A car approached, slowed down and came to a halt. Two soldiers disembarked with their gear and said thanks to their hospitable driver, as he pulled away. They took up position next to me and we talked some, while waiting for a hitch. They were going to Haifa, which was in the direction of Meiron, hence we would be traveling together if a kind motorist would have us. I was actually relieved that they were standing with me, since motorists were more likely to stop for soldiers this late at night than they would for me.

At about nine fifteen an army jeep approached. It slowed down and stopped. He had plenty of room for all of us and we hopped in. I was grateful.

Twelve minutes of dangerous curves later, the driver announced "Meiron." I opened the rear door and hopped down, saying a warm thank you and good night to the thoughtful driver and soldiers, and they were gone.

I was physically spent. I trudged up the hill towards the *tzion*, mustering my last reserve of strength for the expenditure. When I arrived I was astonished to observe that there were more people present than the night before!

"Well hello again!"

I spun around.

"Yoily!"

"Did you just get back from Tzefas?"

"Yes. I got a hitch. And you?"

"I went to Teverya, *davened* by the *mekomos hakedoshim*, had a falafel, and dipped into the Kinneret. I took the eight o'clock bus out of Teverya and got here a few moments ago."

"Yoily, what's going to be? I'm exhausted! If I don't get a good night's sleep, I'm going to break down!"

"The same goes for me. We must find a place for tonight. If not, then I'll have no other choice but to make plans on getting back to Kiryat Sanz tonight. But that would really be a shame, cutting my 'tiyul' short. I would really like to stay on another day or so at the least."

"So let's work at it - together. What about the school building up the hill?"

"I don't think the school building is available any more. You see, the deal is, that the school allows visitors to stay only for Erev Rosh Chodesh Elul. After that they lock up the place. You won't be able to gain entry. Even if you could you wouldn't find a single mat. They must have set up the desks and chairs in the classrooms by now."

"Yes they have. I noticed that when I tried to catch a short nap there today."

"So the school is out. What about upstairs here?"

"Let's check it out."

We ascended the flight of worn stone steps and searched each and every room. Much to our disappointment, every one of the rooms was still occupied. It looked like their occupants would be staying on a couple of days or more.

Frustrated, we descended the stairs back to the courtyard.

"Yoily, did you eat yet?"

"A falafel, and you?"

"I had supper in Tzefas but I'm still hungry. Let's go the kiosk and have a bite to eat."

There wasn't much of a variety to select from, but we managed. Afterwards, we continued our efforts in search of a place for lodging for the night.

"So what do you think Yoily?"

"There just isn't any place available - wait a second - just one second - there is a place! It slipped my mind. Now I remember. Down the mountain path toward the main road, tucked away in a forest, is a cottage."

"A cottage? Belonging to whom?"

"I think it belongs to Rav Usher Freund in conjunction with the community *g'mach* for *hachnossas orchim*. The cottage was filled to capacity with guests this past Shabbos. They should have gone home by now. That means it'll be empty tonight."

"That's great."

"If we get permission to use it, it'll be great."

"Oh."

"I have to locate the one in charge. I'm going to go and look for him. Do you want to come with me?"

"Sure, let's go."

We searched and looked but couldn't find him.

"Yoily, let's go down to the cottage and see what the situation looks like there."

"Good idea," he said.

We proceeded down the dark road, and after some brief difficulty we finally succeeded in locating it. We tried the door. It was padlocked. I peered through the window and saw a large room with about fifteen empty beds. A gold mine!

"Yoily, so many empty beds! Look."

"Yes! What a shame and the door is locked."

"Well we need permission anyway, don't we? Then we'd better obtain the key from the fellow in charge."

"Let's go back up and try to find him. Maybe we'll succeed this time."

We trudged up the hill, exhausted to the edge of our physical limitations. It was nine-thirty. Twenty minutes later and we still had no luck.

"Mutty, forget it. It's no use."

"What are you going to do now?" I asked.

"Go back to yeshivah," he replied.

"Where's that?"

"Kiryat Sanz, Natanya. And you?"

"I can't leave now, I just can't. I must get to Amukah! Through fire and water I must make it."

"But what about tonight? Where'll you sleep?" he questioned.

"I don't know, but I have *bitachon*. Something will come up. I just know it will."

"Well I better get a move on," Yoily said.

"How are you going to get to Natanya, tonight? It's ten to ten. There are no more buses traveling this late."

The rumble of a chartered bus' engine, parked twenty yards from the courtyard entrance, interjected as if to answer my question. Yoily approached the driver and inquired as to his destination.

"I'm taking these people to B'nai Brak," the bus driver declared.

Yoily jumped. Natanya was on the way.

"When are you leaving?" he asked excitedly.

"Ten o'clock," was the driver's reply.

"That's in ten minutes!"

"Correct."

"Can I go along, till Netanya?"

"I'll have to ask the one in charge of the bus rental. Shouldn't be a problem though."

Yoily turned to me, a broad smile across his face, which soon disappeared, when he observed my sad and dejected expression.

"You don't want me to go, do you?"

"Well, if you have no other choice..."

"I really would stay, if I had a place for tonight. Believe me I want to stay another day, to tour the north, but I'm so exhausted."

"Me too."

"So come along."

"I can't. I've decided. I'm staying. Tomorrow's the day for Amukah. You go on along." It was two minutes to ten as we approached the bus' steps.

"You'd better get on the bus, before all the seats are taken," I cautioned.

"There are plenty of seats available and it won't be leaving before ten, I guarantee you."

At ten minutes after ten, the driver announced that he was getting ready to move out. The fellow in charge of the bus said that it was alright for Yoily to come along.

"Should I go?"

"It's up to you, Yoily."

"You won't find a place to sleep. Come along with me," he prodded.

"No, I will find a place to sleep. I definitely will. Hashem never let's me down."

The driver motioned to close the doors and nudged Yoily to make up his mind and fast.

"Nu? Are you getting on the bus or not? I've got to get a move on. It's already ten-fifteen!"

Yoily looked at me, then at the driver and back at me. The sympathy in his eyes was overwhelming. His hesitation and indecision was short lived, as he hopped off the bus steps and declared, "I'm staying!"

"Wonderful," I exclaimed as I slapped him gently on the back. I knew that I would have difficulty getting through the night without his companionship.

The bus shut its doors and slowly pulled away. Yoily looked after it and sighed, "I hope you're right, Mutty."

"I better be right. It's gone now."

We decided to search one last time for the man possessing the key to the cottage. Ten-thirty and still no luck.

"Yoily, one second. What is the cottage used for?"

"*Hachnossas orchim.*"

"That means us?"

"In a way."

"We are stranded with no place to sleep tonight, right?"

"Right."

"Is there a bigger *hachnossas orchim* than that?"

"I see your point."

"We've tried to locate the *baal habayis*, to no avail. Would he mind if we slept in the cottage, knowing that we tried but couldn't notify him of our intentions?"

"Of course not. At least that's the way it should be, if, in effect, *hachnossas orchim* is the actual interest of the cottage's use."

"Then we have no problem, other than gaining entry."

"What are you driving at?"

"We have to find a way to get inside. Let's go down there again and inspect the premises. There must be a way to get in."

We went down the road to the cottage. The door was padlocked as before.

"Is there another entrance around the back?" I inquired.

"No," Yoily replied.

"Let's try the windows then."

Everyone was locked, except for one!

"Yoily, this one here is open at the top! Help me pull it down!"

Together we progressed inch by inch.

"Now how do we get in? It's above our heads," Yoily declared.

"Yoily, I'll hoist you upwards a bit while you try to pull yourself in. Don't worry. I can support you."

Yoily placed his right foot between my cupped hands, as I lifted him upwards. He grabbed hold of the window pane and slowly inched his way in. It was my turn. I got hold of a protruding wooden beam and slowly pulled myself upwards. Yoily grabbed my free arm and assisted me in my climb. Before we knew it, we were in. What an exuberant relief!

"Mutty, we did it! We're in!"

"Boruch Hashem. See, I told you we'd find a place for the night."

The place was totally dark.

"Should we open the light? Should we chance it?" he asked.

"Definitely. Yoily, if we keep the place dark, and somebody comes and finds us here, we'll be accused of breaking in and hiding, like criminals. We must turn on the light. This way we will be demonstrating our total innocence, in exercising our full and inalienable rights in benefiting from the *hachnossas orchim* services rendered to all who seek it."

"I agree," he declared.

He turned on the light, and we suddenly noticed that we had entered the cottage through the kitchen window.

"There's a fridge."

I opened it, to find a pitcher of Kool Aid drink. We filled our glasses to the brim and quenched our thirsts.

"At least somebody should benefit from it," I chuckled.

We moved into the next room. I turned on the light. Beds! Two rows of them. We had arrived! What a joyous moment for both of us. Our precious medicine lie before us. I remember the ecstatic feeling now like it was just yesterday.

"Which bed should I take? This one? Or that one over there? Or maybe this one over here."

"There are over a dozen beds here. It's a hard decision to make. Minutes ago, our problem was finding a bed. Now, the problem is, there are too many of them!"

"This is really something, eh Mutty?"

"I'll write a story about it yet."

A knock on the door cut our conversation short. Yoily and I looked at each other with apprehension and suspense as we stood at attention holding our breath. Another knock.

"Who is it?"

"Open up, please."

"The door is padlocked, didn't you notice?" I informed him.

"Then how did you get in?" he called from the other side.

"Somebody might have padlocked the door while we were in."

"How will you get out?"

"Don't worry about it, we'll get out, somehow. By the way, why do you want to come in?"

"I just wanted to see if I could get a place to sleep for the night."

"You know what? Try to locate the person who has the key."

"Where is he?"

"Maybe up the hill, by the *tzion*."

"Thanks alot."

"Wait a second. Do you want a drink?"

"Ok, thanks."

"Come over by the kitchen window and I'll hand it to you."

He reached up and took the cup from the top of the window.

"Thanks!"

"Don't mention it."

And he was gone.

"I hope he finds another place to stay. I wouldn't want him bringing the *baal habayis* around and, furthermore, I would not mind having this place all to ourselves."

"I don't think we've got anything to worry about. It's already eleven o'clock, and it seems highly improbable that he will have any success in contacting the *baal habayis*. He must be sleeping by now."

Another knock on the door. We held our breath again but this time, the sound of a key being inserted into the padlock, was what we heard, as we stood frozen with fearful anticipation. The seconds seemed like years and after a few moments, the door swung open, as a young man appeared in the doorway.

"Good evening," he said to us.

"Good evening," we replied, hesitantly.

"You must have gotten locked in. How long have you been here?"

"About an hour."

"I'll close the padlock, so that no one will make that mistake again."

"Are you in charge of the cottage," I asked him.

"Not at all. I have the key, as do a dozen others. This cottage has been set aside for *hachnossas orchim*, and I guess that's what it's used for."

"Are you going to stay here overnight?" we inquired.

"No. I'm going back to Yerushalayim in a couple of minutes. There's a car outside waiting for me. I've come to pick up some things. I almost forgot about them. There they are, on that bed. I'll get them and be on my way."

He got them, and as he exited the doorway, said, "Have a good night's sleep!" We thanked him and wished him a safe trip home. Whew! That was a close one. We wiped the sweat from our foreheads, and breathed a deep sigh of relief.

"It's almost twelve, Yoily!"

"We'd better lock and bolt the door and get ready for bed. Do you have your Tefillin?"

"Yes, it's on the kitchen table."

"What time do you want me to wake you up tomorrow morning?" Yoily asked me.

"If you dare!" I said with a smile.

"I was just joking. We'll be up by eight anyway and so we'll make *z'man krias shema*, b'ezras Hashem."

"Of course. If we go to bed now, we can get eight solid hours of sleep and have plenty of time to say *krias shema b'zman*."

We got ready for bed, closed the lights, and tucked ourselves in. Fortunately there was an ample supply of woolen blankets to keep us toasty warm. Yoily and I struck up a conversation, but before we knew it, we were out like a light, knocked down in the first round, at the finish line before we even started.

The next moment I remember, was waking up to the morning light, completely refreshed and rejuvenated. Those were the deepest eight hours of sleep that I had experienced in a long, long time. My *'modeh ani'* was that more vigorous and grateful. What a wholesome feeling! I stretched my delicate limbs, and moaned with pleasure, as I felt myself coming back to A-1 condition.

Yoily began stretching simultaneously.

"Did you sleep well?" I asked him.

"Excellent. And you?" he inquired.

"Couldn't have been better," I replied. "And to think that we almost gave up last night."

"We have to be thankful," Yoily said.

"I tell you, I've never been stranded. Hashem always takes good care of me."

"I see that," he said with a nod.

I glanced at my watch, and my eyes opened wide.

"We'd better get dressed, it's eight thirty, Yoily."

We washed *negel vasser*, dressed, and proceeded up the hill to the *tzion* for davening. After shachris we had breakfast at the kiosk.

"You know Yoily, it's still hard for me to digest that we actually spent the night in the cottage. Without that good night's sleep, we would have been wasted by now."

"Thanks to you, Mutty, I'll be enjoying another full day of touring. If I wouldn't have listened to you, I most probably would have been in Netanya by now."

"Where are you going to tour today, Yoily?"

"I'd like very much to see the Golan Heights along with Har Hermon. I've always want to experience the thrill of standing at the top of it. From there, they say you can see as far as Damascus!"

"That must be some view from up there. I would love to go with you, but you know what I have to do today."

"I know. Amukah."

"I'm going to get on it right away, and this time there'll be no if's, and's, or but's. I'm going."

"By the look in your eye, I gather a team of wild horses couldn't hold you back. I wish you all the luck in the world. Well, I'm going down to the cottage now to get my things, and I'll be right back. I'll meet you at R. Shimon's *tzion* in about fifteen minutes, ok?"

"Sure thing," I said, and he was off.

About twenty minutes later, we met at the *tzion*.

"Mutty, listen to this! As I was leaving the cottage, the *baal habayis* appeared!"

"And what have you been doing here? Whose are those things?" he demanded to know.

"I slept here overnight," was my reply.

"With whose permission? And how did you gain entry?" he asked.

I explained our predicament and thanked him as his *hachnossas orchim* cottage came to our rescue as no other thing could have. He understood and expressed pleasure at having been able to supply two fellow Jews with a place to lodge for the night, but in addition he implied that expenditures in keeping up the place were exhorbitant, and so I understood what he meant to convey."

"Money?"

"Exactly."

"How much?"

"I gave him 200 Lirot."

"I'll give him 200 more for me. He actually deserves it. Who knows, he might let us stay tonight also."

"Here he comes."

I approached him and presented him with 200 Lirot, thanking him for his hospitality.

"Do you think the cottage will be available tonight as well," I inquired.

"Not tonight. We are closing up and traveling to Yerushalayim today. I'm sorry. You'll have to find another place to stay."

"Well, thanks for your hospitality - and one day we'll meet again." We shook hands and parted.

Yoily and I stepped into the little kiosk for a drink, and then back to R. Shimon's *tzion*, to recite a few chapters of Tehillim. Yoily prayed a special farewell prayer at both *kevarim* (R. Shimon's and R. Eliezer *beno*) and then approached me."

"Well I'm on my way, Mutty. It's been a pleasure," and he stretched out his hand. I clasped and shook it warmly.

"Sure will miss you," I said.

"Give me your address in Yerushalayim. Maybe we'll run into each other. Who knows? It's a small world."

We exchanged addresses and phone numbers and bid each other farewell. As he turned to depart, he remarked, "Good luck with Amukah."

"Thanks and good luck to you in the Golan. Enjoy yourself to the fullest."

He walked out of the *ohel* and into the courtyard. As he exited the courtyard gate, I walked after him and was about twenty yards distant when I called out, "We'll see each other again!"

He spun around.

"I'm sure," he waved, blessing me, and continued on his way. I stood and watched as he slowly descended the winding path, until I could see him no more.

I sighed. There goes a true friend, and a devoted companion if there ever was one. I checked my watch for the time. Ten o'clock. My goodness. I had better get started.

Chapter Six

Setting Out To Amukah

The parking lot was full of cars and taxis. I approached one of them.

"Hello, are you by any chance going to Amukah, or know of someone who plans to?"

"No, I'm sorry."

"Excuse me, driver, I see you have a taxi, would you have room for me, to Amukah?"

"I'm not going to Amukah."

"Good morning, are you by any chance passing near Amukah?"

"Not even close."

"I beg your pardon, but are you traveling to Amukah?"

"Not today."

"Sir, could you help me out? I'd like to join your taxi, if you're going to Amukah."

"I'm sorry, but you picked the wrong day."

Frustrated, I lifted my arms in despair. Not to give up. Very important. Never give up. That's what Satan was expecting of me. Well, he was going to lose this battle, with G-d's help.

A taxi pulled up from the main road. I approached the driver as he got out of his car.

"Excuse me driver, I was wondering if you could help me out. I'm looking for a way to get to Amukah."

"Yes."

"Well could you take me there? I mean are you going in that direction?"

"Nobody just goes in that direction! Do you know where Amukah is?"

"I heard it's out of the way and hard to get to, but I was figuring."

"What exactly were you figuring? If you want to rent me, it's going to cost you."

"How much?"

"Twenty dollars."

"Twenty? That's about all I have left for food and my trip back to Yerushalayim."

"I'm very sorry about that, but you must understand, the gas and time, plus the wear and tear on my taxi, due to the bad roads, warrant such a bargain price at the least."

"What am I to do?"

"Why don't you get together a group, and share the expenses between you?"

"That may take some time."

"Well, all you need is four people besides yourself. That'll make it five dollars a piece."

"Twenty five dollars? But you just said twenty!"

"Sure I said twenty. That bargain price is for you alone. I'm not here to rip you off. But if you have people to share the burden, then I see no reason why I shouldn't be entitled to my fair full price."

"I see. You have a point there. Well, can you give me some time to get them together?"

"I think twenty minutes to a half hour should be ample time, don't you?"

"I sure hope so."

"Fine. I'll wait right here. If I don't hear from you by then, I'll be on my way. Time is money you know."

"Yes, I know. Thanks. I'll get on it right away."

Twenty excruciating minutes later and still no luck. Frustrated, I returned to the driver and reported my fruitless efforts. He felt sorry for me. His facial expression portrayed it.

"Don't give up, you'll find the means to get there. The day has just begun."

"That's what someone told me yesterday, and I'm still here."

"Well if you don't have enough money for a private taxi, why don't you check out the buses."

"There aren't any buses to Amukah."

"How about taking a bus to the closest point to Amukah, and then you could take it from there."

"Wait a minute, just one second, you have a terrific idea there! As a matter of fact, I thought about that possibility yesterday, but I couldn't envision how I would go about it. But now that you've mentioned it, I'm going to give a serious go at it."

"See, you're on your way already."

"Thanks, you've been a great help."

"Don't mention it," he said as he got into his taxi and drove away.

A sudden surge of hope swelled up in the inner depths of my heart. A flicker of light at the end of the tunnel finally appeared. Sure! A bus to the closest point near Amukah and then I'd hitch or hike on foot.

I raised my eyes heavenward and prayed that Hashem would help me outsmart Satan in my quest for Amukah.

Ten forty-five. I decided that I would invest another fifteen minutes in trying to obtain a ride to Amukah. After that I would begin making plans for my solo trip to the hidden valley. At eleven o'clock, having experienced no successful results in spite of my persistent and diligent efforts, I began inquiring about the best route that would take me there.

"Excuse me, I would like to travel to Amukah today. Could you tell me how I would go about it."

"I would advise you to rent a taxi, my friend. It's out of the way, at least five miles, from civilization in all directions."

"Couldn't I take a bus to a point nearby and walk from there?"

"Where would that point be?"

"I was told that Amukah is situated somewhere between Tzefas and Hatzor..."

"In a stretch of uninhabitable forest land between those two cities, I might point out, a very dangerous situation to place oneself into indeed."

"Well, if I could determine which of these two cities is closest to Amukah, and obtain clear instructions as how to proceed through the forest, I don't see why I should encounter any difficulty at all."

"I personally do not know which city is closest to Amukah or which paths you would take for that matter, but I strongly suggest you don't go it alone. Your life is too precious to jeopardize in exchange for a hike."

"I'll be very careful, and I'll get there, don't you worry."

"I sure hope so. Well, I see you're set on it. There's no stopping you. I wish you good luck. Put in a good word for me at R. Yonoson's *tzion. Hatzlachah!*" and he turned and left.

I continued to inquire, but no one could tell me how to get there.

The frustration was getting a bit hard to handle. Wasn't there anybody who knew how to get there?

Then I noticed a young boy staring at me, out of the corner of my eye. I approached him. I figured it was worth a try.

"*Sholom Aleichem.* Are you here on a trip?"

"Yes. I'm here with my whole class. We've just been to Tzefas."

"Did you enjoy visiting the *mekomos hakedoshim*?"

"Very much. I've seen most of them two, even three times."

"Have you ever been to Amukah?"

"Sure! I hiked there on foot twice!"

"On foot? From where?"

"Once from Tzefas and once from Hatzor."

"Which one is closer?"

"I would say Hatzor is a bit closer."

"How long did it take you from Tzefas?"

"About two hours."

"Did you have a clearly marked path?"

"Yes."

"How long did it take you from Hatzor?"

"About an hour and a half."

"So Hatzor is definitely closer."

"You could say that."

"Is there a path?"

"Yes."

"Could you explain in detail as to how I would get to Amukah from here?"

"I don't understand. You want to hike on foot, from here?!"

"No, no. I want to take a bus to Hatzor and to continue on from there, either by hitching a ride, if at all possible, or hiking on foot."

"Well, let me think now."

After a couple of seconds of contemplation he said, "You go down to the main road, and take the bus going to Tzefas. It'll stop in Tzefas, to let off and take on passengers. Stay on the bus. It'll continue on towards Rosh Pinna, and then Hatzor. Ask the driver to let you off at the last stop in Hatzor. That'll be as close to the forest as the bus will get. About a hundred yards from the bus stop, you'll see a path that leads into the forest. That's it."

"That's it? I stay on the path all the way to Amukah? There are no forks in the road?"

"No. By the way, there is another path or rather I should say a black-top paved road off the main highway, not far from Hatzor, which also leads to Amukah. That asphalt paved road becomes a tire track dirt road after about twenty minutes or so, and continues straight to Amukah."

"How long will the bus ride take to Hatzor."

"With the stop-over in Tzefas, it shouldn't take you more than twenty minutes to a half hour."

"I better get down to the main road, it's getting late."

"There's a bus to Tzefas at fifteen minutes to the hour, every hour. You can still make it."

"Thanks for everything," I beamed, as I shook his hand warmly and vigorously.

"Have a safe trip, you and your friend," the boy remarked.

"I'm going it alone."

"It's dangerous. You could get lost!"

"I have instructions and it's not as dangerous as it seems. I've traveled alone many times before. Don't worry."

And I was off. I turned to say farewell to Meiron, and hurried down the path towards the main road. I passed the cottage and quickened my pace in the descent. It was twenty-to-twelve when I reached the bus stop, and most fortunate at that, for the bus had just arrived, five minutes before schedule.

I hopped on the bus, my attaché dangling from my left hand, my right grasping a metal bar near the driver for support.

"Are you going to make a stop at Hatzor?" I inquired of the driver.

"Yes."

"Thank you," and I paid the fare.

I settled down in a seat, behind two *B'nei Torah*. I was pensive, so I struck up a conversation with them.

"I'm on my way to Amukah."

They both turned around.

"You are, are you?"

"I can't wait to get there."

"You're going alone?"

"Yes."

"You shouldn't chance going it alone. You can never tell what can happen in the forest. I remember several years ago, hiking to Amukah through the forest, with a close friend. We got lost, and it took us four hours, before we reached Amukah. We were dehydrated. Now, mind you, it was in the middle of April, so you can well imagine the increased danger and hazardous risk you are taking on such a hot scorching summer August day by attempting this hike alone."

"I'm going to purchase soda water in Hatzor. I'll have plenty of fluids along. Besides the hike will only take about an hour and a half tops."

"Well, we strongly suggest, you think it over."

"I've given it thought. I must do this. I've only one more day left to tour, and I'm not going to push Amukah off for the last minute. I want to get it done, the sooner the better."

"Can't you find a friend to go with?"

"How about you two?"

"Don't remind me! When we finally got to the *tzion* of R. Yonoson, famished, dehydrated and totally exhausted, we flopped down near the stone and bemoaned our grave situation. Our tongues were parched dry. If that wasn't enough, the sun was beginning to set! Darkness began creeping steadily over the dense forest."

"Was there no one at the *tzion* when you got there?"

"No."

"So what happened? What did you do? Don't tell me you stayed in the forest overnight!"

"We would have had to, if it weren't for a miracle from heaven."

"What happened."

"I got up from my sitting position, and decided to walk around the stone and lo and behold, at the opposite end of the stone, perched upon the border edge near the ground, were two bottles of "Crystal" soda water, neatly arranged one next to the other."

"Really!"

"I'm telling you, we thought it was a mirage."

"Now that's a miracle!"

"We drank the bottle's contents. Soda water never tasted so good!"

"Well, finish the story. What did you do next?"

"We couldn't, we didn't dare stay overnight in the forest. The cold temperatures coupled with imminent danger of wild animals, induced us to gather up our remaining vestige of energy and strength, and we got out of there."

"Back to Tzefas?"

"That's right."

"You had the strength to walk all the way back?"

"The soda water and brief rest rejuvenated us."

"How long did it take you to get back?"

"About two and a half hours. You see, we had already learned from our mistakes on the way going, so we made good time coming back."

"You said it was getting dark."

"That was the scariest part of our journey back. About an hour and a half into the way it became pitch dark in the dense forest."

"How did you continue?"

"We could still make out the road, although, more than once we stopped in our tracks, frightened, when we thought it had suddenly disappeared."

"That's some story!"

"It had a happy ending, Baruch Hashem. Do you see what we mean? It's just not safe to do it alone. Can you imagine what would have happened to me if I would have dared to try such a foolish thing as going it alone? Please reconsider what you are about to do."

I shuddered for a moment at the severity of his cautious, but well-meant warning.

"You have a point there. I'll try to find someone to take along."

"That's an idea."

"Thank you for your advice."

They both collected their articles as the bus rolled into the Tzefas Central Bus Station. We shook hands and they departed. I would have liked to have taken them along with me on my trip, I thought, as I stared out the bus window after them. Would I have success in convincing someone to join me in my hike?

Several passengers got on the bus, and the driver motioned to leave the station. The bus climbed a steep mountain and exited Tzefas proper. As it winded its way along the serpentine road, I observed the breathtaking scenery to my right down below.

Little did I dream that, one day, I would marry and settle down in these very mountains.

The bus descended very quickly, and was in Rosh Pinna in minutes.

"Are we near Hatzor?" I inquired of a passenger.

"Five minutes," he said.

I checked the time. Twelve ten. Several minutes later the bus came to a halt and the driver called out, "*Tzomed* Hatzor!"

"*Tzomed* Hatzor? The Hatzor junction? That's not what I wanted!"

I quickly scampered down the aisle, to the driver and remarked, "I need to get to Hatzor."

"There she is to the left," he said as he pointed to a community about a mile distant.

"Fine, I'll get off there."

"No, no. I'm not going there. I'm continuing straight ahead to Kiryat Shemoneh. You'll have to get off here and walk."

"But I asked you when I got on if you were going to Hatzor."

"There it is. I don't enter it. I just pass it at the junction. The bus after mine does go in. You should have asked."

"Oh, that's just fine!"

"Are you getting off or not? I have a schedule to keep."

"One second, please! Just let me get my bearings. I need to get to Amukah."

"Amukah?"

"You've heard of it?"

"Maybe. Now will you please get off the bus?"

"Please, please try to understand. I'm lost. Someone has to direct me."

I turned around, faced the passengers and mustered all the courage I could muster, as I pleaded, "Does anybody know in which direction I would have to go to reach Amukah?"

No response. I pleaded once more. Everybody just shrugged their shoulders in apathetical ignorance.

The driver turned to me, impatience flaring up in his eyes, and ordered me off the bus.

"Amukah, Amukah?" I pleaded one last time.

Suddenly, as if out of nowhere, an Arab in a *kaffiyeh* raised his hand and declared, "Wadi Amukah," and pointed in the direction of it. He indicated in broken, crude Hebrew, that it existed in a deep valley, yonder behind the third mountain after the vast plain. I shuddered. It looked more like five miles away!

The bus driver, extremely impatient with me by now, motioned to close the doors and move on. I thanked the Arab, and jumped off.

Chapter Seven

Unbearable Thirst

The scorching, blazing, hot midday sun, characteristic of a typical Middle eastern August day, greeted me, although somewhat impolitely and unexpectedly. The sudden blusterous intense heat affronted me with the strength of a blast furnace. The sky was a dark purple blue, not a cloud to be seen. The sun's rays beat down mercilessly upon me with maximum intensity, as I absorbed the harsh brunt of its unbridled brute strength. Here I was, stranded at a highway junction, under the open sky, vast open plains for miles around, without shade cover or any other type of protection from the sun's strong rays.

Hatzor lie a mile back, down the highway, off a different road junction. The unbearable heat induced me to dismiss the possibility of taking the trek to Hatzor. That alone would take at least an hour, owing to my inevitable sluggish pace due to the raging heat.

To my left, I noticed a black top service road, which seemed to lead from the highway junction towards the direction of those far off mountains. This must be the other road the young lad in Meiron had mentioned, I thought to myself. He did say that there was an asphalt road, a little way after Hatzor that would also lead to Amukah.

Actually, I couldn't be too sure that this was the road or the correct direction for that matter. Might the Arab have deliberately offered me misleading information? Sending a lone Jew off through the forest wilderness in the intent of getting him lost, seemed quite an appealing proposition.

Why hadn't anyone on the bus known about Amukah's whereabouts? Why did he alone seem to possess the information I sought?

I thought it over briefly and concluded that following the Arab's directions was the only option open to me, as I hadn't received any alternative information. I had only his word to go on. It was worth a try. I had come this far. No sense in aborting my mission and turning back now. I would continue on.

I crossed the junction to the other side and began the slow and painstaking trek down the blacktop road. I checked my watch for the time. Twelve-thirty. I raised my eyes to the sun and quickly turned them away in grimmacing pain. The sun was at its zenith. The heat was becoming more and more unbearably intense with each passing minute. I began to perspire profusely. The beads of sweat dripped down my forehead in such quantities that my eyebrows became saturated with them, which caused the spill off to drip into the corners of my eyes. The salty drops stung a bit and I rubbed the perspiration away with my shirt sleeve.

I had gone no more than ten minutes, and already felt the increasing harsh effect of the hazardous and dizzying sun's rays. At this rate, I'd most probably become uncontrollably thirsty in say about fifteen minutes. The body moisture loss was increasing at a rapid rate. If I was to continue on, I would have to do something about fluid conservation and soon. Unfortunately, I hadn't been afforded the opportunity to purchase any soda water. I would therefore have to implement some type of technique to control, and prevent, if at all possible, my rapid body fluid loss which was being caused through profuse sweating.

The attaché case in my left hand. Now there was an idea. I raised it up and placed it upon my head. It provided ample protection from the blazing sun's rays and the immediate change and immense benefit as a result, were instantly felt.

Although having to hold the attaché with one hand proved to be somewhat of a handicap, I dismissed the inconvenience in light of the vital necessity it afforded through its beneficial precious shade. The sweating subsided considerably. I began licking my dry, parched lips, wishing I had taken along water from the start.

The sun was out of my eyes now but began broiling the attaché to the extent that I found it difficult to hold on to it for more than several minutes at a time.

Wait a minute. I was inviting the sun's rays and drawing it to me. Of course! The color black absorbs; white reflects. I opened the attaché, pulled out a white cotton undershirt, and draped it over the case. The beneficial results were immediate. Intuition is a very valuable asset.

I continued down the road. Suddenly a foul garbage stench smell met my nostrils. Where was it coming from, I asked myself. The answer was immediate. The road I was presently on bordered the northern side of a huge garbage dump. Towards my left, for about a distance of two miles, stretched this vast trash site.

The putrid smell, intensified by the decomposing effect of the sun's rays, compounded my already difficult trek. No water, a blazing sun, and a foul smell to top it all off.

The etchings of a faint smile spread across the corners of my mouth, as I remembered that Satan was hiding at the door, waiting to spring in ambush. "Not so fast, evil one. I haven't thrown in the towel yet. I'll make it, *b'ezras* Hashem. As long as I still breathe, you'll have to muster up your best weapons to combat me, and by all means, I do not wish you good luck!"

With inspiration, renewed strength and rejuvenated vigor, I continued on my way, in spite of the tremendous efforts expended. The lack of water to quench my extreme thirst, the harsh trash odor which was making me dizzy, and the terrible heat spell which was compounding that dizziness, made it some what difficult for me to walk a straight line.

But as always, that small flicker of light at the end of the dark tunnel miraculously appeared. I had finally reached the northwestern edge of the dump site and the horrendous odor would soon be behind me.

And what's this? A tire track path, branched away from the black top road, towards the left. Could this be it? Did the boy mean this road? I checked my watch for the time. One o'clock. It had taken me approximately twenty minutes from the highway junction to get to where I was standing now. The boy did mention that a tire track path would appear to my left, about twenty minutes down the black top road. And I noticed that the dirt road gradually curved towards the right and continued in the direction of those far off mountains. Everything pointed, "This way to Amukah" or did it? I couldn't be one hundred percent sure. The road I was presently on also seemed to be going in the direction of those mountains, the only difference being, that it curved towards the right first and then left as opposed to the tire track road which curved first to the left and then to the right. Both roads seemed to be leading to the same destination, just utilizing different routes in getting there.

Should I perhaps stay on this black top road a little while longer? Might there be another set of tire tracks up ahead which the boy meant for me to take? Was I being too hasty in wanting to take this fork in the road?

I placed my feet together, put my attaché on the ground, raised my eyes heavenward - and prayed. Several moments later, I had the strong feeling and inner urge that my destiny lay down this tire track road, to the left.

Decision made, I bent down, scooped up my attaché, and placed it upon my head. Then I draped the cotton undershirt over it as I began the trek of a somewhat uncertain journey down a mysterious and adventuresome looking trail.

The trail curved slightly to the right, winding its way around a small hill, and suddenly, I found myself standing before a vast olive tree grove. There were literally hundreds of olive trees, sprawling to the right, left and in front of me, for as far as the eye could see.

The grove, a flat plain about two hundred yards wide, was nestled between two hills which bordered on her right and left perimeters. The tire track path, consisting of two parallel gullies, winding and curving moderately side by side, entered the grove and became hidden from view.

The young lad hadn't mentioned anything about running into an olive tree grove. He might have figured it was irrelevant and impertinent, since the tire track path was all I needed to know. I sure hoped so.

"Well, here we go," I whispered to myself, as I began the journey, and entered the grove. The path weaved through clusters of trees, taking me on a fantastic nature tour of sun-ripened olives. I picked a few and studied them, their texture, color and aroma. I hadn't seen ripe olives on a tree before, so this was a first.

I continued on. The sun was beating down, mercilessly blazing away in all its intensity. I licked my parched lips yearning for a drop of water to quench my intolerable thirst. Checking my watch for the time, I noticed that I had hiked only thirty minutes yet it felt like I had trekked for hours.

The dryness in my mouth, the dizziness in my head, the dust on my face, clothing and shoes, all contributed to the hardship and difficult decision of whether to continue on, or to abort and go back home.

Satan again. Ah yes, he would stay close behind, did I forget. Don't give up so easily. Give him a good fight. A smile spread across my mouth as I lifted my feet and continued on my way. Amukah it is and

Amukah it will be. I'm not a quitter.

The path weaved through the olive trees, casually. The approaching curves were hidden from view by the dense trees of the grove, making each progressive step that more adventurous and anticipatingly suspenseful. I did not know what lay fifty feet ahead of me. And it was quiet, very quiet. Just me and the wilderness interacting and cooperating with each other. Complete silence. Very still.

Then, all of a sudden, a noise! I froze. There it was again. Somewhat like a muffled grunt. Slowly and steadily I turned my head around towards the left until my eyes met up with the sight of a tall and powerful majestic ram, sporting the largest spiral horns I did ever see. Standing his ground upon the top of the hill, adjacent to me, I noticed that he was staring inquisitively at this strange intruder who had wandered into his private domain. I stood frozen in my tracks. What was I to do? I was afraid to move. He might charge me. I motioned to place my attaché case on the ground, and as I did, he jerked suddenly. I stood frighteningly still, trembling, but keeping my composure, as best I could.

Then it came to me. If you sing to a wild animal you relax it. Music makes animals complacent. I began humming a tune. He cocked his ears, moving his head from side to side, a quizzical expression on his face all the while, studying my presence and the strange sounds that were emanating from my mouth. The seconds turned into minutes. I must have stood frozen at attention for about ten minutes before I decided to make my daring move. I motioned to bend down towards my attaché, and just as I did, that huge animal gave the largest jump, I ever saw, and in a fleeting instant was over the hill and gone from sight. Glad he didn't jump my way. Whew! That was a close one. I wiped the beads of perspiration from my forehead, replaced the attaché upon my head, and gave a blessing of gratitude and thanks to the *Ribono Shel Olam*, for standing over me and protecting me from perilous danger.

Checking my wristwatch, I noted that I had already spent an hour on my journey, which meant I had about a half hour left to go, according to the calculations of that young lad back in Meiron.

Strange, but there was as yet not a sign nor even a marker of some sort, hinting that I was on the right way to Amukah. One would surmise that at least one symbol would be posted along the path to enable a hiker to know that he was indeed heading in the right direction, and not just lost somewhere in the middle of nowhere.

The thought of getting lost in the forest expanse did not appeal to me. I abruptly dismissed the frightening thought of that possibility and continued on.

My hands were becoming tired and fatigued from holding the attaché up, so I decided to forgo the benefit of its shade, removed it from upon my head and carried it in the regular fashion. The sun's blustrous rays immediately bathed my forehead with its intense heat, and my dizziness increased doublefold.

I placed the attaché back upon my head, and decided that I would have no other alternative but to forgo the comfort of being able to place my hands down at my side, for the benefit shade that the attaché afforded.

The path continued its winding way through the olive grove. As I turned a curve, I was horrified by the frightening sight of what lay before me not more than ten yards away. Directly on the tire track path between the parallel gullies, the grotesque remains of a partially decomposed cow's head, eyes intact, open and staring right at me, sent shudders and chills up and down my spine. Terribly horrifying. Flies were swarming all around it. I couldn't, I didn't dare continue on straight ahead. Its wide open eyes staring angrily at me really scared the living daylights out of me, almost as if the head was alive and holding me responsible for its demise. Even its mouth seemed ready to open at any moment to scold me for its tragedy that I was in no way responsible for.

Everything was still. Deathly silent. Literally. Not a sound to be heard except the thumping of my heart beat.

What to do. I had to get a move on. Another quarter of an hour or so to go, according to my watch. Almost there, according to that young lad. I gathered together my remaining courage and strength, and followed an alternate path which circumvented the unappealing sight, and which returned me to the original trail. Sure glad to have passed that tribulation. Enough shocking experiences for one day!

I doubted whether my exhausted and dehydrated condition would allow for the absorption of more of the same. It frightfully dawned upon me that this wasn't the safest place to find oneself in. Being all alone in the wilderness was proving to be hazardous and dangerous. I should have hearkened to everyone's cautious advice. I should never have tried this daring escapade, alone.

But what is done is done. I would have to make the best of it. Onwards. I raised my right foot and trudged on. I became weaker and thirstier with each painstaking step. What I wouldn't have given for a glass of sparkling cold, refreshing water. Just the thought of it caused me indescribable anguish.

The sun kept beating down, my parched lips enduring the blusterous heat with a mustered last ounce of strength. I checked my watch for the time. I should have been there by now, or at least have experienced the sighting of a sign of somewhat. Yet, in spite of my hardship, turning around was out of the question. Onwards.

The tire track path continued its gentle weaving through the olive tree grove, until...what's this...no, it can't be...just not possible. The path suddenly came to an abrupt end! I rubbed my eyes in disbelief. The tire tracks curved one last time and terminated up ahead about twenty yards distant. A crude barbed wire fence, a field of tall thorns and brush just behind it, marked the end of my road.

A cold hand of fear gripped my trembling heart, as I was positively certain that I had gotten lost, and would, unfortunately, have no other recourse but to turn around, and attempt the tremendous effort of returning to from whence I had come. I looked down at my shoes, which were a shiny black before I had gotten off the bus. They were covered with dust now. Slowly and steadily I raised my eyes toward the road behind me, and just sighed. Going back would take me at least an hour. I hadn't the strength for that, especially since the thought of having come this far for naught, would definitely compound the pain and physical exhaustion that I would have to endure all the way back to the road junction.

I came this far, I would continue on. There had to be a way to Amukah. Somewhere near by. I must have made a slight miscalculation. But I'd find it. I just had to. The barbed wire fence. Some type of clue, an existing hint of some sort, which would open up my way. Yes! There towards the right, I noticed a slight opening in the fence, which indicated that someone before me had indeed passed through, not withstanding the considerable difficulty entailed in such an act. But to where? The fence bordered upon a dense thicket of tall thorns and thistles. Could anyone have possibly entered and traversed through that? And if perhaps a brave individual did succeed, in what direction did he continue? A large steep hill presented itself directly in front, some ways after the field of thorns. If I could get through the thicket what then? Where to next? Up the hill would there be a road? Would I have the strength?

Only Hashem could help me decide. That was the constant rule! An inner surge prodded my being. It clearly insisted, I must go - proceed - continue. Try my best. Trudge onwards. With my attaché in hand, I bent carefully and eased myself through the tailor-made opening in the barbed wire fence. Then the pain began. The clusters of sharp thorns and thistles scratched and scraped at my shirt and pants. Oh the pain! Trying to avoid the brush by pushing the thorns away with my hands proved futile. My hands and face absorbed scratches and scrapes and I groaned under each onslaught. I decided that it would be best to just run through the tall thicket and get it over with.

About thirty seconds later, I found that I had suddenly emerged from the dense, tortuous thicket, and astonishingly observed that I was now standing once again before a tire track road! Miracle of miracles! It had materialized as if out of nowhere.

My heart rejoiced as I gave thanks to *Hakadosh Boruch Hu* not withstanding my thirst and exhausted condition. In spite of the fact that it was late, and that I was most probably on the wrong tire track road, still, all of these shortcomings were seemingly forgotten and pushed aside to make room for the abundance of joy and thanks that permeated my heart.

I began to walk upon the tire track trail which began its ascent up the hill. The going was obviously very slow, but I continued steadily, raising my eyes periodically, taking note, of my progress. Stopping to catch my breath, I turned around and scanned the panorama of the plain in the far off distance below from whence I had come. I recognized the main road, where I had gotten off the bus, by the cars that were streaming to and fro, and noticed that it must have been close to three miles away. There was no feasible way, in my present condition, to have even contemplated a possible return trek to that highway. Onwards.

I took a deep breath, and continued the uphill trek. Several moments later; the unexpected. The tire trails' final termination jostled my complacency. The end. This time the trail had actually retired for good. Or so I thought. The tire track path did terminate itself, true, but a couple of yards distant, a narrow, single-lane path took up where the tire trail left off. That was a consolation. At least there was hope in a guided continuance of some sort. Slowly and steadily I climbed higher and higher, turning around intermittently to observe my altitude in contrast to the highway on the Hatzor plain way down below. The view was breathtaking.

Onwards. Each step became more and more difficult to take. The physical strain and immense thirst began taking their toll in leaps and bounds. Dizziness started setting in. Lights began flashing on and off. And then, to top it all off, the single path suddenly and unexpectedly branched off into three directions! What now. The stakes became suddenly much higher. I stood still in my tracks scratching my forehead as I observed the grave situation before me. One path branched off to the right and upwards. A second path branched off towards the left and upwards to a second mountain, and a third path continued straight away at first and then began curving in a serpentine fashion upwards towards the summit of the mountain which I was presently on.

I distinctly recalled the Arab's words: "Over that third mountain, in a deep valley, lies the valley of Amukah." This summit before me, was the first in that row of mountains, and it seemed most probable that the path which would traverse the summit would most likely be the proper trail to take. Yet, the other two paths couldn't be ruled out. Actually, I couldn't be too sure that this mountain before me was at all the definite first in a row of three. Perhaps it was very possible that when the Arab had pointed to the mountains in the far off distance, he could have meant the ones on either side of her, and that would really place me in a complicated dilemma.

I placed my feet together, raised my eyes heavenward, and prayed to Hashem. Tears swelled up in my eyes. "Hashem, I am thirsty. I have no strength left. Have mercy upon me. Please grant me the wisdom to enable me to choose the proper path."

I stood at attention, eyes tightly closed, my face raised toward the blue sky, as my thoughts concentrated on salvation from above. A couple of moments later, I opened my eyes. Scanning the three paths once again, my thoughts surmised and contemplated, weighed and measured the probabilities and possibilities, until, with the aid of Hashem Yisborach, I chose to continue upon the middle path which ascended the mountain before me. True, it states in the *seforim* that when one encompasses a fork in the road, and knows not in which direction to continue, he is advised to take the road to the right, but in this case, the road to the right seemed to be leading away from my final destination, and back towards the direction from whence I had come.

I drew a deep sigh of relief, having arrived at a definite decision in taking the middle upward path, but before continuing on my way, I knew that my body sorely needed a rest. From about twelve o'clock to three-thirty, I hadn't stopped even once to relax my aching muscles. I would faint if I didn't stop to rest a bit.

Several yards off the path, I noticed a large stone, and so I sat my weary frame down upon it. Every bone and muscle ached and throbbed, thanking the stone for its hospitality.

My mouth was parched dry, my face, shirt and pants covered with dust and thorns. I sized up the situation and drew a broad smile. An adventure was at hand, most probably a test to measure my *bitachon* in the Shepherd of the world. Yet I had brought the test upon myself. The broad smile was therefore tinged with a semblance of trembling seriousness. The fact was that I was presently immersed in a grave situation, which I alone had caused. No one forced me to go it alone. On the contrary. I was forewarned, again and again. I had no right to have embarked on such an expedition by myself.

But the stark fact remained. Here I indeed was, and some way, somehow, I trusted that Hashem would spare me and bring me to eventual safety. Now, all that really mattered, was expressing my deep faith in Hashem and to believe that He would forgive my shortcomings, especially this one here, the mistake of having set out all alone.

As I rested, my eyes began to scan the immediate area around me. On the ground, a mere two feet away, I observed a display of thousands of ants, who were busily removing particles of thorns from a hole, which seemed to be an entrance to their ant colony. A steady stream of them flowed to and from that hole, constantly transporting bits and pieces of grass and twigs. With swiftness and extreme diligence they continued their activities, not stopping even for a moment's rest. I was transfixed by their actions. I marvelled, "How great and wondrous are Your works Hashem!"

I sat there watching intently for about five minutes, and suddenly asked myself, why Hashem had directed my eyes to this unusual display of diligence and commitment. As always, I knew that everything in Hashem's world was placed in it for a specific purpose, to teach a lesson of some sort, or to direct one's thoughts and attention to a certain situation. What was I to learn from these diligent and hard working creatures? Of course! Couldn't I see? Two specific lessons were to be learned here: One, that my service in *Avodas Hashem* should one day resemble these creature's zealousness and diligence; and two, provided that this message is well taken, I could look forward to experiencing success in my journey to Amukah, if I would but continue on, not losing hope, just as these creatures kept continuing on in their activities. The important message in other words was, "Don't despair. Continue on down the road. Keep it up. You'll make it. Don't give up!"

And so, with a renewed surge of hope, my body experienced a sudden burst of energy and I felt myself being somewhat rejuvenated.

It was getting late. Time was moving on. Slowly, and steadily I pulled myself up off the stone, and stretched my aching limbs. Holding my attaché firmly in hand, I continued the upward climb, on the middle path. About a quarter of an hour later, another fork in the road appeared. Upwards I continued on the same middle path, higher and higher, enduring the extreme physical strain with as much fortitude as I could. As I climbed, the perspiration poured and my mouth became drier with each advancing step. Acute dizziness began setting in and lights started flashing on and off as before. I felt faint. "Hold on! Hold on!" I reassured myself. "Look up, you're almost three quarters of the way towards the tree-covered summit. It shouldn't take too much longer to reach it," my heart echoed. Could I reach it? The uphill trudge quadrupled my already strained efforts and it seemed therefore impossible to envision that I could accomplish such a feat. But I had no other choice, no other option open to me, other than continuing on aided by the last remaining reserves of my determination. I trudged upwards, dragging my feet slowly, pitifully, pausing intermittently to catch my breath.

Raising my eyes upwards, I was relieved to notice that I was now very close to the summit. About a hundred yards or so left to go. Swiftening my pace, I began scampering upwards, in the intent of getting it over with, but alas, who was I kidding? I began gasping deeply, trying in vain to catch my breath. And then...I collapsed...not fainted mind you, just flopped wearily to the ground. My head was burning and my eyes were bloodshot. I felt the throbbings in my head, and placed my hand to my forehead, massaging it gently, trying to ease the pain. I began drawing deep gushes of air into my tired lungs.

Several minutes later I turned my head gently to the right, where my eyes were surprised by what they beheld. Was it a mirage, or did it actually exist?! I raised my head a bit more to get a better look, to make sure my eyes weren't playing tricks on me. No, it was definitely there. Glory be! A wide dirt road! I had collapsed near the edge of a road! My heart swelled with thanks, as I sat near the edge of the dirt road, anticipating the generosity of a kind motorist.

'Wait a minute, just one minute,' I said to myself, as I scanned the road up and down. There were tracks, tank tracks, the length and breadth of her. Army tank tracks! It gradually dawned upon me that this road here, as perhaps others throughout the forest dense, was most probably set aside for military exercises and maneuvers. It wasn't a public road. I could sit a week before one of those tank contraptions rolled by.

I would have to continue on. No sense in sitting and waiting for the sun to set. I decided that I would walk upon the tank track road, using it as my current guide. But that decision wasn't too clear or final matter-of-factly, for the road contained two directions, one to the right and the other to the left. And I still had the option of continuing my ascent up the mountain and over its summit, in the intent of continuing straight ahead as the Arab had instructed. This option proved unappealing, though, as my strength gauge for "uphill progress" read "empty."

Here again, my indecision as to what I should do, called for the most appropriate saviour, namely that of earnest prayer.

Chapter Eight

Lost in the Forest

The decision of preferring to stay on the road, rather than climbing the summit, owing to the probability that by staying on the road, I could possibly chance to meet up with a motorist, where in the forest I could not, proved to be an excellent deduction, yet worthless in content next to the faculty of earnest and heart-rending prayer. Entreating Hashem, crying out to Him from the depths of my heart, this method surely surpassed all others.

And so once again, I placed my feet together, closed my eyes, and turned my face upwards toward the sky, in fervent prayer. Several moments later, I opened my eyes, breathed a deep sigh of relief and felt the decision enter the innermost chambers of my heart. 'Continue on the dirt road towards the right,' it insisted. And so, I picked up my attaché and began trudging through six-inch deep, fiery red dirt, barely dragging my feet along. Every step, deplenished what ever miniscule strength I had left. It was no less than a miracle that I could still continue on.

I began to feel the effects of the sun's rays, once again, as the flashing lights began popping on and off, in front of my eyes. I had to get out of the sun and quickly, so I decided to hug the left side of the road, which afforded a sparse amount of shade, owing to a couple of trees here and there. About a hundred yards down the way, the road forked into three directions. One to the right and down, seemingly going away from Amukah, towards the direction from whence I had come. Another one straight away, and down into an extremely deep and dark valley. And the third, branched off, towards the left, circumventing the mountain side towards what might have been what the Arab meant to convey, when he pointed with his finger towards what he said was "Wadi Amukah." This latter road which curved towards my left, ascended for about a hundred yards or so, and then dropped steeply into the forest's depths. The road to my right was immediately dismissed. The road in front of me and the road to my left, both held me in suspenseful indecision. Could the road directly in front of me perhaps be the golden path to Amukah? It did descend into a very deep valley. Yet the road to my left in kind, although it first ascended a bit, likewise began its long descent into the forest's depths. An added complication to my indecision was the fact that by embarking upon either of these two roads, I would be moving farther and farther away from civilization, descending into the forest dense.

Prayer. The only option. I raised my eyes heavenward. "*Hakadosh Boruch Hu*, my thirst is unbearable. You gave Shimshon water, when he cried out. I too, am now crying from the depths of my heart. Have Mercy! I request a gift of kindness, for I know that I am not deserving of your beneficial Grace. Have pity on me and hear my plea! Hearken to my weak and trembling voice, and direct me upon the right path, for I cannot hold out much longer."

The stark silence of the forboding forest, its mystical enchanted bliss, disturbed by the sudden outburst of an entreating voice, crying out from the depths of a human forest, densely populated with trees of emotion and feelings, rooted by a rock of solid trust, seemed a rare occurrence indeed. The echo of my crying voice, aroused the inner emotions of my spiritual conscience, sending chills up and down my spine.

And then everything stood still. Even the birds kept their silence. It was as if everyone was waiting for Heaven's reply. The trees kept from swaying. The wind stood at attention. Not a sound to be heard, other than the faint echo of my breathing, and the subtle gentle thumping of my heart beat.

And it was in fact my heart that received the anticipated reply, as my eyes turned towards my left to face the road, which beckoned me to her.

With heartfelt gracious thanks, I bent to pick up my attaché and began the continuation of my excruciating journey. Step by step, I dragged along, wondering how I was actually able to do so. It felt as if someone was helping me along, pushing from behind. Like a robot, placed into motion, programmed by someone's electrical instructions.

Upwards, the road climbed at first, making my progress that more difficult. Here unfortunately there was no shade from the blistering sun's rays, and so the intense sudden heat compounded the already unfortunate situation at hand. But a sweet consolation was, that the road's ascent would soon be short-lived as I could already see the spot where it would begin its descent. Just a little bit more to go. A little extra effort and the uphill trek would be behind me.

It is impossible to convey on paper the excruciating pain, that these last steps entailed. Let it suffice to say that it must have been an angel, who lifted and carried me those remaining uphill yards.

At last, I had reached the point of descent. I took a deep breath standing for a moment, to observe the road's forthcoming descent. All of a sudden, my eyes caught sight of what seemed to be a wooden sign, several yards distant off the road to my right! Eureka! A sign! Directions, at last! Well it was about time.

I scampered hurriedly over to the sign, as a renewed surge of strength permeated my being, confident that the sign would inform me about Amukah, of course. But as I got closer my heart sank in bitter despair. The sign read: Keren Kayemet L'Yisrael – The Jewish National Fund. This forest has been dedicated by Mr. and Mrs. Schwartz of Chicago, Illinois.

I just stood there, in dismay. I couldn't believe it! Amukah, the holy resting place of R. Yonoson ben Uziel, was somewhere in this dense forest and directions to this revered place, should have, in all logical consequence, overrided any and all issues pertaining to this forest. Yet the monies that Mr. and Mrs. Schwartz of Chicago, Illinois donated to the State of Israel, took precedence.

"Thank you Mr. and Mrs. Schwartz," I declared. "Now how about donating some money for a meager sign which would point the way towards Amukah?" I chuckled. It was fortunate that I could still chuckle, still find a source of humor to keep me in good spirits, to hold me back from getting depressed and losing all hope.

Oh well, it was good while it lasted. Now, to carry on with the task at hand. The road's descent. It seemed like it didn't have an end. It just kept on going deeper and deeper into the forest's depths, and then disappeared into dark oblivion.

I knew very well that once I began the downward trek, I would have to continue on with no turning back. It would be downhill all the way, and no coming back up under my own power. That could very well mean having to remain in the forest overnight if I didn't find my destination by nightfall. I shuddered at the frightening thought.

What would I eat or drink? Plants and wild berries came to mind.

Sucking out the juice of a leaf, as I had read in a book about self survival. Where would I sleep? Rodents and snakes, wild animals, terrorists, too much for my mind to handle. I quickly dismissed these terrible thoughts, deciding to look at everything optimistically. I'll get there before sunset, I kept on telling myself. And even if I didn't, I'd meet someone on the way. Standing here, under the broiling sun, waiting for it to set, was surely no solution. And so I bent down, picked up my attaché and continued the journey.

I glanced at my watch. It was a quarter to four! Terrible thoughts of "a short-lived life, due to transgressions," "this is the last day of my life," and "I shall never see the face of a human being again," kept creeping back into the frightened chambers of my conscience.

My mouth had reached its "nth" degree of dryness. My legs felt practically no feeling. But I continued on for their was still hope. As long as I breathed, salvation was very much a concrete possibility. The dragging of my feet grew more difficult with each painstaking step. The fact that I was descending, did not help to ease the pain and suffering in my legs. A soft bed, a cold refreshing drink...Oh the pain of the thought!

And then, suddenly I raised my head, and beheld in the distance a wooden sign. My heartbeat quickened. I forced my feet to hasten, but alas they just wouldn't, rather couldn't, respond. My desire was to reach it quickly, and so I expended an extra effort, in the hope of being rewarded by its wonderful news, but as I came closer, my heart sank as did the road. The words on the sign had now come into full view: "This forest was donated by Mr. and Mrs. Cohen of Los Angeles, California." "Very good! Wonderful! Exactly what I wanted to see! That Mr. and Mrs. Cohen donated monies for this quaint forest! I am extremely overwhelmed! Thank you Mr. and Mrs. Cohen! But why isn't there a sign showing the way to the holy resting place of R. Yonoson ben Uziel!!! Not that I'm belittling your beneficiality, Mr. and Mrs. Cohen, but still in all, if you would both stand here at attention, directing travelers to Amukah personally, instead of donating a costly sign with an arrow, at least that would be something."

A little spice of humor to lift my downtrodden spirits. I needed it badly. My eyes moved away from the sign, as my legs continued their seemingly endless trudge upon a mysterious road, which appeared to be descending to the center of the earth itself. And the lower I got, the darker everything became. It was as if the sun was getting ready to set over the horizon any minute. I checked my watch for the time. Four o'clock. Sunset wouldn't be for another three to four hours. But in the forest dense, especially in its deep valleys, sunset could readily fall in less than a couple of hours!

Onwards. The strain. Unbelievable suffering and excruciating pain. When will it all end? When will this journey finally be over?

Suddenly I heard something in the distance. A faint drone of an engine. It was getting closer and louder. Then I caught sight of a Volkswagon, white in color, on a road, way down below, whisping through the trees.

Almost immediately I began yelling for help, in the hope that I might be heard above the din of the powerful engine, but it was no use. They didn't respond. The road which the Volkswagon was travelling upon way down below, was most probably an extension of the same road that I was on. Patiently I observed its progress, but then it was gone and the sound of its engine began to diminish. The road down below must have continued on straight ahead into the forest's domain and the motorist chose to continue on down that road.

The disappointment was great. To have been so close.

Onwards. My rate of descent did not slacken. Deeper into the caverns of the forest, brought deeper shades of darkness. The sun was beckoning its rest.

To hear the sound of a human voice, civilization, anything! The acute silence was frightening and forboding. I continued to descend, deeper and deeper as it got darker and darker. Finally I noticed, that I had reached the point of the road where it joined up with the road that the Volkswagon had taken.

Dragging my body along the way, my thoughts began drifting to the cherished memory of my dear departed father, *olov hashalom*. How I missed him! I guess the sadness of being alone in the forest caused me to think of him, for when he left the world I truly started feeling alone. This road was long, hard and difficult, as was his life; and lonely.

My mind was so preoccupied with these thoughts that when a signpost came into view, about a hundred yards distant, I didn't notice it. As I stopped to wipe the sweat from my forehead, it caught my eye. Quickly, I removed my glasses, wiped the dust off them frantically, placed them back into position, and squinted trying to make out the sign.

I advanced toward the sign. Closer and closer...as my eyes squinted to make it out. I could now see a red arrow pointing to the left. And then...black Hebrew letters, crudely painted. As I got closer the letters began taking shape...I removed my glasses, and placed them back on. I took them off again, rubbed my eyes vigorously, and again placed them back on my nose. The sign read...no it couldn't be...too good to be true...but it did...the sign clearly read: "R. Yonoson ben Uziel - Amukah," with a red arrow underneath. My heartbeat surged and began racing uncontrollably, and a lump formed in my throat. It was true! Yes! It was true! My eyes began to water. The tears flowed down my sun burnt cheeks. I checked again to make sure my eyes weren't playing tricks on me. The sign was still there. I placed my attaché at my feet, raised my eyes heavenward and began crying tears of joy. A renewed strength afforded me to raise my voice in song, as I shook the forest with the sudden burst of my majestic tenor, inherited from my father. The entire forest, the heavens, and the creatures abounding in them heard my prayer of thanks.

Chapter Nine

On the Right Path

I must have stood there for about ten minutes, eyes raised heavenward crying with uncontrollable joy. But the joyous tears soon gave way to saddening ones as I began remembering and recalling the memories of my sweet father, of blessed memory. "Tatti! What a treasure was lost to me! If I would have only known! I went to learn Torah in Yeshivas Lakewood at your insistence. Could I have realized that you really needed me at your side? O forgive me for I was not aware of the realities." And the crying intensified. The tears flowed and waterfalls of emotion washed away the impurities of the heart.

Gradually, the pent up anguish and pain slowly released itself from the shackles of the innermost depths of my conscience, bringing a cease to the flow of tears. I wiped the salty teardrops from the corners of my eyes, a mixture of sweat and dust, which stung slightly, and continued on. As I did, my thoughts involuntarily traveled back to the memories of my father, and I began to sob once again. Taking control of myself, I forced the emotions to lay dormant. I needed strength to continue on.

As I neared the sign, I noticed that it was situated at a fork in the road. To the right of it, a narrow dirt road continued into the forest and to the left of it, actually more straight ahead of it, lay the road to Amukah, as the sign's arrow clearly indicated.

Slowly and painfully, yet with a sense of exhaustive accomplishment and joy, I passed the sign. Again, the memories of my beloved father, permeated my subconscious causing me to groan from the depths of my heart. I convinced myself that he had just gone on a long vacation, so to speak, and that I would surely have him back soon with the advent of Moshiach and *Techiyas Hameisim*. Yes, I would be consoled in the very near future.

I continued down the dirt road. In the distance, approximately fifty yards away, it looked like another fork in the road. What now? There was no sign around. Could it be? After all this effort, there was an imminent danger of getting lost again?! "Clear your head," I said to myself. "Don't give up." I prayed to Hashem to grant me wisdom in order to enable me to decide the direction that I should continue with. Seconds later, my brain began functioning with uncanny skill. This road here branched off, towards my right and down, into a deep valley. Amukah? Not likely. The sign back there clearly indicated that the road I was presently on, was the proper direction towards Amukah. If the intended purpose was to change directions, namely, by getting off this road, then it would have been logical to expect a sign at this very spot, indicating that such action be taken. As there was no sign present, it seemed apparent, almost obvious, that continuing straight ahead on the present road, would be the proper action for me to take.

I bent down, picked up my attaché and proceeded forward. At least I was comforted by the realization that I was better off now than before I had encountered the sign to Amukah. Prior to it, I didn't know where I was, or if I would live to see tomorrow, which thus intensified my fear and thirst, as one lost in the desert, not knowing where he presently is, or if he will ever experience an end to his pitiful travail, experiences similarly, a much harder affliction during his excruciating trek.

But now that I was in the right direction to Amukah, it didn't really matter how much longer it would take. I was on my way. My situation reminded me of an analogy in conjunction with two types of people: One of them believes in the coming of Moshiach and the inherent termination of our bitter exile, and the other one does not. The former one suffers less pain than the latter one, for he who believes and trusts that there will inevitably be an end to this bitter exile and that peace, tranquility and joy will reign supreme in the days of Moshiach, automatically experiences a drastic reduction in his affliction; his pain and suffering become lightened considerably, similar to the man who finds it markedly easier to endure his suffering and wanderings in the desert, because he knows beyond the shadow of a doubt, that an oasis is only several miles away.

But, heaven forbid, he who does not believe in *Bias HaMashiach*, is like the man who wanders in the desert aimlessly, not knowing when and if at all his travails will end, which in fact intensifies his suffering manifold. We have two people here traveling under the same sun, and in the same desert, yet one reduces his suffering merely by the sheer will of his belief. I, similarly, felt a drastic reduction in my pain and suffering, since the sighting of the sign to Amukah. This alleviation of nervous fear, gave me the strength to continue on.

Several minutes later I heard the faint but definite drone of a car's engine. The car came into view, around a bend. It was a taxi. I raised my free arm and waived to the driver, signaling him to stop. I wanted to inquire if I was indeed still in the right direction towards Amukah. He didn't make any effort to slow down and stop, so I placed myself smack in the middle of the road, which brought his car to an involuntary halt.

The windows were closed, protecting the passengers from the dust without. I approached the driver's window. He just stared at me, utterly amazed.

"Pull down your window, please," I said to him.

"I don't have any room for you."

"I don't want a seat."

"What do you want?"

"Pull down your window will you."

He rolled down the window, slowly, carefully, cautiously...and stared disbelievingly up and down at me.

"What is it then?"

"You must tell me, you just must."

"What?"

"I've been in the forest close to four hours."

"What did you say?!"

"I've been wandering on foot for almost four hours, under the sun, without a drop of water."

"Please, please! What are you saying?!"

And everybody began rolling down their windows, to see and hear what this was exactly all about. They peered inquisitively at me.

"Yes. I've walked from the Hatzor junction."

"I don't believe you! I'm sorry, but I just can't."

"But I did! Look at my shirt and pants. Look at my tongue."

My shirt was black, my pants, white, and my tongue drip dry.

"But where are you headed," he asked.

"That's why I stopped you. Am I headed in the right direction to Amukah?"

"Yes."

"Yes!"

"It's back there, a little ways."

"Oh Thank you!"

"Just continue on. It's about another ten minutes. Look, I gotta go."

"Thanks," I said, as he started to roll up his window and move on. The passengers eyeballed me in disbelief, muttering to themselves. They even turned around in their seats and stared at me from the rear window. When they were finally out of view, I let out a whoop and a yell. I was almost there! It was true! I breathed a deep sigh of relief as my heart thanked Hashem for His gracious salvation. Everything would be fine now. Just fine. I was so overwhelmed with joy. I did it. I was closing in on the home stretch, the finish line.

My legs, suddenly rejuvenated, raised themselves and began a slow but steady and deliberate walk.

Chapter Ten

Amukah at Last!

A good fifteen minutes later, and there, down below...there it was! A miraculous sight to behold! It was as if an unbelievable and spectacular dream had materialized out of the clouds in the sky. Amukah at last! Tears welled up in my eyes, as I rejoiced and let out a cry of thanks. I had finally reached my destination. I could rest my weary eyes upon the holy *tzion*, and utter a prayer. This was happening. It was real. I kept at it and didn't give up, and I was rewarded. I finally made it.

I stood still for several moments, observing the holy *tzion*, the people standing nearby, who were praying, and the general area with its exceptionally impressive fauna and breathtaking scenery. What a mysterious and mystical setting, for a place such as this, I thought. A hidden valley, tucked away somewhere, in the deep recesses of a mystical wonderland, protecting a precious treasure from the multitudes of the cities and towns. It was as if it was reserved only and exclusively for the privileged few who would take it upon themselves to expend the painstaking effort in undertaking the journey to the *tzion*.

I waved my hand high above my head and caught the attention of one of the visitors standing near the *tzion*. He waved back. I proceeded to descend towards the *tzion*, and noticed the many steps, which led from a small dirt parking lot to the *kever*. It reminded me of the interesting story that lay behind the construction of those steps. I had heard about a young single man who, while praying at the holy *tzion*, professed a vow, promising that if he would find his mate within the year, he would see to it that stone steps be placed all the way to the *kever* (as the only way to approach the *tzion* was via a steep and dangerous, narrow dirt path). He married within the year, and the steps were constructed. Well over a hundred of them!

For the evil ones, the path is smooth and easy in the beginning, but rough and difficult in the end. The righteous ones however, experience a rough time at the beginning, but smooth and clear sailing in the end. My journey was painstakingly difficult and harsh at first, yet smooth and polished towards its culmination, paved by these very steps, polished stones donated by a righteous young man, whose difficult journey going it alone, was blessed with a helpmate to accompany him through the wonderful journey of life. A very important lesson learned here in addition, was that every significant accomplishment in life, warranted a constant vigil, a consistent persistence, in defying all odds that be, suppressing and defeating any and all subtle feelings of sadness and depression, rising above the mundane pursuits of the evil inclination, and finally succeeding in attaining true happiness and joy in the service of Hashem. With the help of Hashem Yisborach I overcame and succeeded. I had arrived, as had the fortunate one, who married and donated thereby, the many steps, which would aid others in their arrival. Everything, every aspect of life, contains a lesson.

The same white pickup that I had seen, whisking through the forest earlier in the day, was down below in the parking lot area. When I got there, I approached the people standing near their pickup requesting water to quench my unbearable thirst.

"Excuse me, but would you have some drinking water available? I am very thirsty. I've just journeyed through the forest, close to four hours."

"What!?"

"Please, I've come all the way from the Hatzor junction. Please give me water."

"What did you just say?" he exclaimed looking me up and down in disbelief.

"If you don't believe me, just look at my face and observe my clothes. They're saturated with dust. My mouth is parched dry," and I stretched out my tongue.

"Come on! Do you expect me to believe such a story!"

"Please, I beg of you, I have no strength to talk," I whispered with a tired and drained pathetical voice.

His eyes scanned my pitiful frame up and down, and suddenly he broke into a run towards his friends. "Yossy! Shimee! Listen to this! This person says he's been through the forest four hours, under the blazing sun, without even a drop of water! He says he's come all the way from Hatzor. From the junction!"

His friends stared at me from afar. And then one of them reached into the back of the pickup, withdrew a rather large plastic container of water, handed it to the fellow who had spoken with me, who in turn ran with it back to me. "Take! Take! Drink!"

He turned to the others who were now approaching, and called out, "Look at that! He journeyed close to four hours through the forest, all the way from the Hatzor junction, in order to reach Amukah! Isn't he a saint?"

Then he turned to me and said, "We are all *baalei teshuvah*, and we would be very interested to learn all about Amukah and the holy *tzaddik* R. Yonoson ben Uziel. I and he; he's my brother, and him, well he's my cousin. And this one here is my son. Say Shalom to the Rabbi."

"Give him to drink! He's thirsty! Give him a little time to rest!" his brother interjected.

"Yes, yes, I'm sorry, I didn't think. Here take. Drink."

"Thank you," I said, taking the jug from his hands. I made a loud and clear *berachah*, raised the jug's spout to my lips, and began to drink. I drank and drank as they stood transfixed in awe watching the uncommon spectacle. I paused for a moment to catch my breath, and then raised the jug's spout back to my mouth and continued. In a matter of minutes I had emptied the half-gallon to the last drop.

I held up the empty jug. They looked at it, unbelievably, scratching their heads.

"Now we really believe you!"

We all proceeded down the numerous steps to the *tzion*, and when we reached it, one of them turned to me and asked...

"What's your name?"

"My name is Mordechai Menachem."

"That's a very nice name; Shalom, Mordechai," he said, as he stretched out his hand and shook mine.

Others began gathering around and upon hearing of my feat, they began questioning me in detail about the journey.

"Boruch Hashem, you're here. That's what matters."
The *baalei teshuvah* resumed their conversation with me.

"Tell us please, all about R. Yonoson ben Uziel. About his greatness and holiness."

I recounted to them the words that were engraved on the stone:

"When R. Yonoson learned Torah, any bird flying over his head, would be burnt instantly!" I continued with the Gemara in Megillah 3a: "The translation of the Torah was written by *Onkelos HaGer*, of the Prophets, by R. Yonoson ben Uziel, and thus the land of Israel quaked an area the distance of four hundred parsangs squared. A heavenly voice proclaimed, "Who is the one who dared to reveal my secrets to man!" R. Yonoson b. Uziel stood on his feet and said, "I am he. But be it known to Thee that neither for my own honor or for that of my fathers' did I do it, but for Your honor O Lord, to avoid conflicts." He wished to reveal a translation of the Scriptures as well but a heavenly voice rang out and proclaimed "Enough!" What is the reason, asks the Gemara. "Because it contains the issue dealing with the Messiah's coming. And Rashi expounds: In the book of Daniel."

"In other words," I continued, "It is apparently evident that R. Yonoson ben Uziel knew the exact moment of the Moshiach's arrival and the resulting termination of Israel's bitter exile! He knew the secrets that were locked up in the Scriptures! And this my friends, is most probably the reason why he is buried here at this very spot, and why they call this place 'Amukah'. R. Yonoson ben Uziel knew the secret of Moshiach's exact moment of arrival, which Hashem did not want him to reveal through his translation of the Scriptures. He was therefore destined to be buried in a secret out of the way, valley ('Amukah') a very deep one, hidden and extremely distant from mankind and civilization, for the fact remains that the secret of Moshiach's exact moment of arrival, still remains very deep 'Amuk' and far removed from all of us."

They were genuinely moved by what they had just heard. After several moments of contemplation, they requested of me to bless the young boy. I felt unworthy of such a request, but they repeatedly insisted and so, I placed my right hand upon his head, closed my eyes and concentrated as I blessed him. The father of the lad said, "Thank You. Now please stand near the *kever*; I'd like to take a picture of you. I must show it to all of my relations and friends." I declined, and emphatically so, but to no avail. His strong will, and sincere entreaty, overpowered me and I succumbed to his request. I stood reluctantly near the *kever*, and struck a pose, as he snapped my picture.

Everyone then turned toward the holy *tzion* and began praying in earnest. About twenty minutes later, I was asked by one of the people present, "Why are you praying? Can it be possible that a person such as you, should have problems? You are surely a saint. What could you be missing that warrants such fervent prayer?" After a curt explanation, I returned to my praying, concentrating with heart and soul.

Several minutes later, the *baalei teshuvah* announced that they would be readying to travel back to Teverya, momentarily. They offered to take me to Tzefas and I gladly accepted.

We kissed the *kever* and proceeded up the steps back towards the parking lot.

On the steps, we encountered an elderly couple with their son, who were on their way down to the *tzion*. The *baalei teshuvah* began recounting my story to them, and they portrayed wonder and amazement. The elderly man inquired, "How old are you? Are you still a *bachur*?" I replied in the affirmative and he said, "Then *l'fum tzaara agra* - according to the toil and suffering is the reward - Surely now you will find your *zivug*." I smiled and confirmed his blessing with a loud "Amen!" and we continued our climb towards the lot.

We reached the Volkswagon, and filed in. I sat in the back of the pickup with two of them, and settled down, as the driver started up his motor.

Chapter Eleven

Tzefas

After a bit of really rough riding, we emerged upon a black top road. Moments later, the Volkswagon came to a gradual stop, as the driver announced, "Tzefas!" I collected my things and carefully, descended from the back of the pickup. I shook everyone's hand and reverberated with a warm genuine thank-you to all present, and the Volkswagen slowly pulled away. Well, I did it. Amukah was past me.

I proceeded upwards to Rechov Yerushalayim, walked it full circuit, all the way around the city, and finally came to rest my weary body down upon a quaint wooded tourist bench, at a look-out area, which afforded a breath-taking view. It was as if I was high up in the cleft of a rocky cliff, looking down upon a sea of hills.

At the opposite end of the bench, sat an elderly well-kept gentleman. We struck up a conversation, and before long we were talking about anything and everything. History, Religion, Psychology; the Orthodox as opposed to the irreligious. He was a trial lawyer, robbed of a spiritual Torah education. The dialogue became so complex and in-depth, that when we glanced at our watches, two hours had elapsed! In spite of that, he wanted to continue on, for I could sense that he was terribly thirsty for Torah wisdom which he was diligently extracting from our intriguing dialogue. I answered his questions with patience, understanding and forbearance.

As it was getting late, almost time for mincha, I excused myself politely and we shook hands vigorously. As I turned to leave, he called out, "It has really been an exceptional experience to have conversed with such a scholar, a young one at that, and I thank your for your patience and precious time. Be blessed!"

"The pleasure was mine, really. I hope that my Torah words will have left the proper impression, that you will think things over and adjust your life goals and aspirations accordingly. Shalom and *kol tuv*."

"*Shalom u'vracha.* Success in all your endeavors!"

I noted that I had about an hour to sunset, and so I decided to take a mini tour of the Old City, its quaint alleyways, and antiquated holy shuls. The Abohav Shul, that of R. Yosef Karo and the Alshich.

After my brief tour, I glanced at my watch and saw that it was time for mincha. I proceeded to the Ari shul. Entering this wonderful place of worship, I sat my weary body down and marvelled at the magnificent *Aron hakodesh*, truly a work of art!

Congregants began assembling for prayer, and one of them announced that there would be a *chuppah*, taking place, on the *bimah*, after maariv. That would be interesting.

As I waited for the *shliach tzibbur* to begin mincha, my tired and weary body began talking to me. I was physically spent, hungry, thirsty and exhausted. I had trekked through a forest, close to four hours under a blazing middle eastern sun.

Shemoneh Esrei was difficult. The maariv *Shemoneh Esrei* even more so, but I made it.

Immediately after maariv, I sat my weary body down upon a convenient stone corner bench in the courtyard, and waited for the bride and groom to arrive. While waiting, my thoughts began contemplating where I would spend the night. Meiron was out.

Sitting on my right, also waiting for the *chuppah*, was an elderly man. He said *Shalom Aleichem*, and we struck up a conversation. I talked of my ordeals and activities of the day, and that I was from America. That last item did me in.

"Have you a place to stay?" he asked.

"Not really," I replied.

"Well you could stay by me tonight," he added.

"Oh, why thank-you," I said.

"I only take take two-hundred lirot per night," he added.

"That's, that's quite reasonable," I barely managed to say. Why did I tell him that I was from America? I had but three-hundred lirot in my pocket! Two-hundred for him; thirty for supper (I would try to get the most out of just thirty); and that would leave seventy, of which fifty I would need for my trip back to Yerushalayim! Oh well, I wouldn't beg for a hand-out - a free night. It was rather an awkward feeling, to say to someone who had just named his price, that you are really a poor, needy American. Fine, two-hundred lirot it would be. What's done is done.

"Thank-you kindly. I will be coming tonight. But first I must have supper. I haven't eaten since this morning."

"Where will you eat supper?" he asked.

"I was thinking of the Aishel Restaurant, down Rechov Yerushalayim."

"Have a good meal. Here is my address," he said as he handed me a note with his address on it.

After the meal, I reached the bus stop, and was surprised to see my host with his little boy standing there, waiting for the bus to come. We greeted each other. He voiced concern about the bus being late. It was already nine o'clock. A passerby had informed us that the last bus had been at eight-thirty, and that we would have to walk.

"Walk?!"

"It's only twenty minutes, " the host said.

"But I'm so tired. I don't know if I can make it."

"Twenty minutes, that's all. I do it practically every other day."

"I guess there's no other choice."

We began walking. Twenty minutes later I complained, "Are we there yet?"

"Soon, soon, " he assured me.

Then we began walking uphill. The second half of our trek was just straight up. I was upset. I didn't realize he needed the two-hundred lirot that bad! I was subjected to a total of forty minutes of pain, even after I had told him of my ordeal to Amukah, and how exhausted I was!

Finally we reached his apartment, and I was shown to my room. I asked if I could take a shower. I was saturated through with caked-on dirt. My clothing was a muddy mess too. I wanted to wash them. Listen, for two-hundred lirot the least he could give me was some hot water and some laundry detergent.

"Here is your room," he said. "Would you perhaps prefer to sleep in the other room with my son? He already is so attached to you."

"Oh no, thank-you. This room will do just fine," I assured him. I washed my clothes by hand with cold water and took a cold shower. You know - the water boiler takes four hours to heat up, and electricity is no bargain. Cold water it was, brrrr! But it felt good to be clean.

The next morning, I awoke, a bit refreshed, and took the building elevator down to the first floor to the shul for shacharis. After shacharis, I took the elevator back up to the apartment. In the hallway corridor, several yards from the apartment, I met the same man who had blessed me with, a *zivug b'meherah* on the steps of Amukah just the day before!

"Are you the young man I met on the steps of Amukah just yesterday?" he asked.

"Yes, what a coincidence."

"Where are you staying?"

"At Mr. Friedman's apartment, down the hall."

"Are you staying on for a few days more?"

"I'm not really sure about my plans. Today is Wednesday. I might stay on today, and travel back to Yerushalayim tomorrow afternoon. I would still like to tour the Old City."

"Listen, I have a very special girl for you, she's divorced true, but she's a very fine girl, believe me, exceptional character and very attractive. She's about your age. Do you want to see her? She's presently in the building right now."

I stood still.

"Now this is the problem," he continued. "I am travelling to the airport tomorrow, for my trip to America, and she is leaving for Yerushalayim tomorrow. In two weeks time she is planning to travel back to America. See her here, now."

I was still in a state of shock. Did he say divorced? See her now?

"I...I'm very sorry, but I haven't a suit or a hat. All I have is what I'm wearing, and look, look at me. My pants and shirt are still full of stains! I cleaned and washed them last night by hand, but look, they're still somewhat dirty. I must wash them in a machine. I can't see a girl without clean clothing."

"Don't worry! Listen to me, you look just fine. I know what I'm saying. Go and see her today. Here's her phone number. Take it down and call her, or if you like I can speak with her now, and you can see her today in around two hours or even less."

"Truthfully, I'm very sorry, but it isn't proper if she saw me this way. The first impression is always of paramount importance. Believe me, I just can't."

"Alright, I think I see your point, but how will you get to see her? She is leaving to Yerushalayim tomorrow, and I do not know where in Yerushalayim she will be staying....do you have a telephone number?"

"I can give you my number in Yerushalayim, although I do not quite believe that she would call me."

"She might just call."

I gave my phone number and parted with Shalom. I was still quite in a daze. Had he said divorced and see her right now? Too fast, too quick. Yet on the other hand, I had met him in Amukah. And now meeting him here, with an opportunity relating to a *zivug*. Who could say for sure, how the clocks and wheels of fortune were turning.

I continued to the apartment, knocked, and the Mrs. opened the door.

"Good morning, would you like some breakfast?" she said.

"Oh thank-you but, no. I'll get my things and be on my way. I've got a lot to see today."

"Well how about a glass of orange juice at least."

"That'll be just fine."

She poured me a glass and I downed it thirstily. I thanked the Mrs. telling her to thank her husband in my name, and departed with Shalom. I took the elevator down to street level, got on a bus, and got off several stops later near the Old City. From there I walked down to the *Bais Hachayim*, and became absorbed in my prayers at the various holy *kevarim*: The Ari z'l, Reb Moshe (his son), R. Moshe Kordevero, R. Yosef (Ridbaz), R. Shlomo Alkebatz (Lecha dodi), The Tosfos HaRid, The Alshech (Toras Moshe), The Navi Hoshea Ben Be'ari, R. Moshe Matrani (Baal HaMabit), Baal Bee'r Mayim Chaim, Baal Arvei Nachal, R. Yosef Karo (Shulchan Aruch), and many more.

At about one in the afternoon, saturated with heat and holiness, I proceeded to the Mikva HaAri. It is said that it has been flowing in the mountain since *Sheshes Yemei Bereishis*, and that its source is *Gan Eden*. Furthermore, anyone immersing in her spring waters, is assured that he will not depart this world without having done *Teshuvah*.

It took me around twenty solid minutes to enter her icy cold waters. Little by little, inch by inch, not like the last time, when people chided me to jump in and I did, only to experience, bells clanging and lights flashing on and off in my head. This time, I did it ever so slowly, gradually, wisely until I conditioned my overheated body to the freezing waters. This way it wasn't cold at all, and I stayed in close to twenty minutes.

I emerged, rejuvenated, and totally refreshed. What a pure, clean and wholesome feeling. I felt like a new person. Someone present mentioned that it was beneficial to drink the clear spring water, from where it flowed out of the mountain rock. I bent down and drank till I had my fill. It was deliciously cold and sweet.

Afterwards, I visited the "Ari Shul", a four hundred year-old stone building, where the holy Ari had officiated as Rav, and where he learned with Eliyahu Hanavi. I tried the door but it was padlocked, and so I peered through a glass window. "How terrible and frighteningly holy is this place!" I whispered to myself. I later learned that it was closed the entire year, due to its extreme holiness, and only once a year, on the Ari'zl's *yahrtziet,* ten old and wise men, gathered to pray at this very, holy shrine.

As I prayed, the mysterious wind whistling through the centuries old olive tree above my head, I did not dream that I would one day actually settle down and make my home but a few minutes walk from this holy shrine.

I proceeded up the mountain slope until I reached the Old City. Then I made a circuit of the Old City shuls again.

As I was immensely hungry, I decided that I would purchase a falafel and a drink, but first I had to check just actually how much money I had, remaining in my pocket. I still had to get back to Yerushalayim. Counting the coins, I was relieved that I had enough for a falafel, two drinks and my transportation back to Yerushalayim, and about ten lira remaining.

After the falafel and drink, I proceeded towards the scenic lookout and tourist bench, where I had met the trial lawyer the previous day. I sat myself down, and enjoyed the beautiful, breath-taking view.

Time for mincha. I proceeded to the Ari Shul (built upon a field, where the Ari and his *talmidim,* greeted the Shabbos queen, every Shabbos eve), and waited for a quorum to assemble. After mincha, I decided that since I hadn't enough money to pay for an overnight stay, I would have to rush to the Central Bus Station and catch a bus to Yerushalayim, via either Teverya or Haifa. But I didn't want to leave Tzefas just yet! Tomorrow would be Thursday. Another full day of touring, just one day ahead. What a shame! I was already up here in the Galil. I had another free day. But how could I stay? I hadn't money for food or lodging. I would have to leave.

Dejected, I walked the alleyway, from the shul's central courtyard, towards the steps that would lead me upwards to the main throughfare, where I would take a bus to the *tachanah mercazit.* Wait a minute! I had an idea. Who said money was the criteria for staying another day? I had a plan...

"Excuse me, do you know if I can still catch a bus to Yerushalayim via Teverya or Haifa?"

"Well...I...I don't actually know," he sheepishly replied.

"You see, I'm really in a bind. I must get back to Yerushalayim today since I haven't enough money to buy supper and overnight lodging in Tzefas..."

"Oh, I see..."

"So, I must know if I can still catch a bus."

"Mmmm."

"Do you think I can still make it?"

"Well...I'm not sure...let me ask. 'Excuse me, is there still a bus to Yerushalayim today?'" he asked someone.

"I don't know," the person replied.

"Oh well, I better get a move on," I said.

"Mmmm..."

"Shame. I wanted so much to stay on, for another day of touring, but alas what can I do? I haven't the money."

"Mmmmm..."

"Do you happen to live in Tzefas?"

"Yes, I do."

"Are you married?"

"Yes."

"Children?"

"Yes."

"Oh well, that's nice. Guess I better go now."

"Mmmm..."

"Now, if I would have a place to stay over tonight... you know, just for one night."

"Yes...if you had a place. Let me ask this fellow here...he...he's a good friend of mine..."

"Moish, do you have room for a guest tonight, or do you know of someone?"

"No, I'm sorry," Moish said.

Then Moish said to the dreamer, "One second! You have place and plenty of it! Your wife and kids are in Teverya. Why don't you take a guest in to sleep in your apartment? That way, you won't have to sleep alone."

I couldn't believe my ears. This guy was really one for the books! Here, he was all alone in an apartment, with an opportunity to have a guest to keep him company, and he had no idea who could put me up for the night!

"You're all alone?" I exclaimed.

"Well...yes."

"Why?"

"Well, uh... my wife is expecting any day now, so she went to her mother in Teverya to have her baby."

"So you're all by yourself. You know you're not supposed to sleep alone."

"Oh...I...I guess you're right. I was thinking about it today. You're right. What should I do?"

"What should you do? No problem! I'm willing to stay at your place and keep you company. It's a big *mitzva*."

"But...but I don't know."

"Why not? What's the matter?"

"I don't have anything to serve you for supper."

"What's the big deal! A little bread and butter, some salad, a leben and a drink and there you have it!"

"You...really don't mind?"

"Of course not!"

"Well then, I guess its okay."

"Of course it's okay! You've got yourself a guest," and I shook his hand.

After maariv, we went to his apartment. He took out some frozen fish, fried it and served a rather delicious meal. I found conversing with my host quite difficult, as he seemed to be constantly in his own dream world. It really made me very nervous and tense. After supper, he showed me his artwork.

Then we retired for the night. Actually, he retired. I was in the bathroom practically the entire night, with acute stomach cramps. I was up till the morning daylight. My head was heavy, my stomach full of excruciating cramps.

Slowly and carefully I went to shul, but continued to suffer. After shacharis, I lay my aching body down upon a wooden bench, holding an unsteady hand to my sweating forehead. I was very weak and very disappointed. I had wanted to utilize the day for touring, but now this. I had planned to finish seeing the Old City and then to go on to Hatzor to Honi Ha'Me'agal's *kever* and then to Teverya. The last bus to Yerushalayim was scheduled to leave from Teverya at seven o'clock.

Laying on the hard wooden bench, I began praying with all my heart for a *refuah sheleimah*. A half hour later, I found that I could raise my head ever so gently. Slowly and steadily I worked my way back to my host's apartment, thanked him for the 'wonderful' fish, and departed.

Slowly now. Steady. Every sudden move sent sharp pains through my aching head. There was no time to wait for a bus. There would be only one every hour. I couldn't afford to waste precious time, so I began the long and painstaking walk to the *tachana merkazit*.

Upon arrival, I bought a ticket to Hatzor and waited for the bus to arrive. I inquired of the person next to me.

"Excuse me, but do you think I have enough time to travel to Hatzor and visit the *kever* of Honi Ha'Me'agel, take a bus back here; transfer for a bus to Teverya to see the *mekomos hakedoshim* there, and still be able to catch the bus out of Teverya to Yerushalayim at seven?"

"I would like to think so, but it doesn't seem likely. Theoretically, if you could catch every bus, on time and to the minute, you might make it, but that's cutting things rather short. I would suggest that you take a bus straight to Teverya and forgo Hatzor."

My head began throbbing. My stomach was acting up again.

"Please, Hashem, give me the strength to continue on and make it to Hatzor."

Chapter Twelve

Back to Yerushalayim

At about one p.m. the bus to Hatzor rolled in. I decided to take my chances and got on. We arrived at the Hatzor junction at about one twenty. Memories of Amukah came to mind. There, not too far away, was the garbage dump site, and the black top road. And the far off mountains, hiding Amukah. That was some experience.

The sun was blazing away as it did the day before, and was affecting my headache for the worse. I had to get under the shade of the trees at the side of the road.

I inquired of a passerby to direct me towards Honi Hame'agel. He said that I would be wise to wait for a bus, which would take me to the end of the long uphill avenue, where I would then continue on by foot, upon a narrow dirt road, at the forest's edge. I would then continue upon that road for about five hundred yards, till the holy *tzion*.

Surely, now there would not be enough time to get everything in. Then a car stopped unexpectedly, and the driver motioned that I could hop in for a ride. Great.

"Where to?" he asked.

"The *kever* of Honi Hame'agel, or as close to it as you can possibly take me."

"I'll take you even closer to it than the bus would. You'll still have to walk a couple of hundred yards or so."

"Thanks. Thanks for your considerate help."

My head and stomach were still very heavy. The intense heat in the car made me nauseous. The driver reached the end of the town, right near the forest's edge, and I departed saying a hearty thanks.

It was almost two p.m. Would I still be able to make it? Could I possibly still hope of reaching the seven o'clock bus out of Teverya?

I had the uphill trek ahead of me, several hundred yards or so, to Honi Hame'agel's *kever*, with my terrible condition to make matters worse. Then I'd have to backtrack to this spot, and wait for a bus back to Tzefas. The ride would take at least half an hour. In Tzefas, I would have to wait around, who knows for how long, for a bus to Teverya. The ride itself would take about an hour. That would mean arriving in Teverya at about five p.m. or even later. Would I have enough time to see the *mekomos hakedoshim* over there, such as Rabbi Meir Baal Ha-Ness and the Rambam, and still have enough time to make the last bus out of Teverya at seven?

I began the uphill trek into the forest and twenty minutes later, I was praying strong and hard at Honi Hame'agel's *kever*. I kissed the sacred stone and departed. As the way was now downhill, I found it much easier to progress. Also my head felt fifty percent better. I reached the forest's edge in about ten minutes. I checked my watch for the time. Three p.m.- could I still make it?

The bus stop junction was about a mile down the avenue. It would take me at least twenty to thirty minutes to get there on foot. "Hashem, please give me strength to continue on. I'm so weak."

And then suddenly, as if out of nowhere, a bus appeared, not more than 100 yards distant and stopped. Wait a second, I thought. Why walk to the junction? I'd catch this bus to the junction and save precious time and strength! Of course! I broke into a trot, hoping the bus wouldn't pull away before I got there. When I had only several yards left to go, the bus began to move! I waved frantically, hoping the driver would see me, as I continued my dash. He was getting ready to turn the corner, when finally he caught sight of my frantic waving and stopped. I approached the door, panting heavily...

"Yes?" he said.

"Are you heading in the direction of the Hatzor junction and on to Tzefas?"

"No. I'm heading straight for Teverya."

"Teverya! Did you say Teverya?!!"

"Yes. Via Rosh Pina."

"I don't believe it, it's a miracle!"

"Are you getting on, I haven't all day."

Slowly and steadily with the help of the bannister, I pulled myself up the steps, holding my stomach, with my free hand. The sudden dash to the bus intensified my pains, yet the sudden unexpected joy helped to offset much of the discomfort. It was hard to believe! Hashem had heard my entreaty. I requested grace and He hearkened to my pitiful voice. Straight to Teverya!

I paid the driver and as I looked at him, I recalled that I had seen him somewhere before.

"You look familiar. Aren't you the driver who took me yesterday from Har Canaan to Tzefas?"

"I certainly am. I remember your face. How are you?"

"Well, I'm a little under the weather, but listen to this..." and I began recounting the events.

He raised his eyebrows, and chuckled a bit, commenting that it was really something divine.

I settled back in my seat and began contemplating the activities and happenings of the past five days. The unofficial engagement also came to mind. Her father's blessing was to have come over the phone from America, that Sunday evening, hours after I had departed for the North. Today was Thursday.

I drifted off and took a nap and when I woke, we were fast approaching the waters of the Kinneret. At three-thirty we pulled into the *tachana mercazit*.

The intense blusterous Teverya heat and humidity compounded my uncomfortableness. I proceeded to the information window and inquired, "When do the buses go to Yerushalayim?"

"Every hour. Four, five , six and the last one is at seven."

"Do I have enough time to tour the *mekomos hakedoshim* and still get back here for the seven o'clock bus?"

"Where would you like to go?"

"I would really like to go to visit the *kevarim* of R. Meir Baal Haness, and the Rambam at the least."

"There's no problem with that. Here, I'll show you. You exit this building and take the number "five" to R. Meir Baal Haness . It'll take you about fifteen minutes. After that, you'll take the number five on the opposite side of the road for the return trip back here. Once here, you can walk by foot, only ten minutes or so, in that direction (he pointed), to the Rambam's *kever*."

"Thank - you very much."

Outside the Central Bus Station I waited for the number five. It arrived, I got on, and approximately fifteen minutes later, I was standing at the foot of the hill, to R. Meir Baal Haness. I ascended the very steep hill slowly, as I was still rather weak. I was famished and thirsty, yet I didn't dare eat or drink for fear of my weak stomach and the consequences of the pain afterwards.

I davened mincha, and prayed fervently for Hashem's eternal blessings. It was about a quarter to five, when I departed the holy edifice, and descended the hill to the road. Crossing it to the other side, I found myself standing in front of the Teverya hot springs. I noticed a bubbling fountain, in the courtyard garden, a refreshing drink I thought, so I approached it and placed my right hand into the fountain pool. It was a hot spring!

The number five arrived at the *tachana merkazit* at about five p.m., and I proceeded directly to the Rambam's *tzion*. I figured on getting back to the Central Bus Station before six, so that I could take the six o'clock bus to Yerushalayim. I prayed at the Rambam's *kever*, and at the others in the quaint garden nearby: Rav Ami, Rav Asi, R. Yochonon ben Zakkai, R. Yehoshuah ben Chananiah, Rabbi Shimon ben Netanel, Rabbi Elazar ben Arach, Rabbi Eliezer ben Horkonos and the Shiloh Hakadosh.

About twenty minutes later, I set out for the *tachana merkazit*. There were many people at the station waiting for the six o'clock bus and I began thinking about waiting for the seven o'clock one, as I wasn't sure that I would be able to get a seat on the six o'clock one.

The bus rolled in, and the passengers filed on. I took my chances and stood in line. The driver closed the doors right behind me and pulled out, but it was already too late: standing room only! He packed us in like a can of sardines!

I felt sick. It would be a good three hours to Yerushalayim. Standing!!! Quickly I weaved through the crowd in the aisleway, and reached the rear door exit. Hurriedly, I sat myself down upon the top step and breathed a deep sigh of relief.

I had a seat, true, and I was thankful for that, but alas the stifling heat at my level became unbearable. To make matters worse, I was getting nauseous from looking out the rear door window at the scenery rushing by. I began sweating profusely, holding on with all my remaining endurance.

At about nine p.m. we reached the heights of Yerushalayim, and the brisk, crisp night air refreshed my senses. At the *tachana merkazit*, I took a local bus to Geula, and walked the couple of minutes to my apartment on Rechov Malachi.

I rested for a good hour. Then I got up, *davened* maariv, had something to eat, and retired for the night.

Friday morning, the next day, I got up early, and *davened* shacharis. Coming back to my apartment, I noticed a message by the phone indicating that my eldest brother had called to invite me for Shabbos.

Friday evening, I was his guest at the Shabbos table and I recounted my adventures.

After Shabbos I went to visit my best friend.

"Shalom Aleichem! I've come back from the Galil. I was back Thursday night, but I needed Shabbos to recuperate."

His face was drawn.

"What's wrong? Why are you so sad?"

"Why I'm so sad? Do I look it?"

"You sure do."

"I think you should have a seat first, before you hear what I have to tell you."

"What are you talking about?"

"It's off."

"What?"

"Yes. It didn't materialize."

"What happened?"

"Sunday night she called her father in America. I was there near the phone when she called."

"And..."

"He said 'nothing doing.' He would not give his blessing unless he saw the prospective candidate first."

"He expected you to jet to America?"

He added that even if I did jet to America he would not agree to any tems whatsoever with regards to helping me out so that I could remain in Kollel. I spoke with the Rosh Yeshiva and he advised me to give it up as the reality for the continuance of learning seemed remote."

"This is such a shock to me. I feel so bad for you."

"You don't know how much I needed someone to talk to. The whole week I was looking for you but then I remembered you said you'd be going up north. No one could really understand my pain. I was so depressed. I stayed confined to my room for three days."

"That's terrible."

"I'm glad you're here. Finally I can talk to someone."

"Start all the way from the beginning."

We talked for about two hours. He unloaded as much as he could. His feelings, her feelings; the realities involved. Everyone got hurt.

He began breathing a bit better and managed to even smile a little.

I knew too well the feeling of rejection, of the hurts and emotional scars, the complicated and misconstrued intentions and the futility of trying to live up to unrealistic expectations.

I assured him that it would take some time and patience coupled with forbearance, and it would finally pass. The blessing of time accrues the forgetting of pain.

Chapter Thirteen

The Phone Call

Several days later, I received a phone call in the evening at my apartment.

"Hello."

"Yes. Who's this?"

"Is this Mordechai Reich."

"Yes, it is. With whom am I speaking?"

"I was in Tzefas last week and my relative told me that you had seen me there and that you were interested in meeting me. You even gave your phone number, instructing him to give it to me so that I should call you in Yerushalayim."

My mouth dropped. She really called!

First of all, I decided telling her that I had never seen her, but that I would meet her. She did call; I had to agree to see her. We were to meet at the Plaza Hotel.

"I'm really surprised that you're actually here," she said in the hotel lobby.

"Why do you say that?"

"Well, to tell you the truth, you are the first boy I've met since my divorce. I am a bit nervous. No one wanted to see me since, because of my situation."

"I can understand your pain. People are afraid of divorce, I guess."

"Are you?"

"It's not a question of being afraid, but rather of analyzing the situation at hand. I would focus on the future and concentrate on the hopes and aspirations that lie ahead."

I would have to handle her very gently. Great care would have to be exercised not to hurt her feelings in any way.

"Would you like something to drink?"

"Why...yes, thank you."

"A coke or a sprite. Or perhaps an orange juice."

"I would prefer something strong. A hard drink if you don't mind."

"Excuse me?"

"You know...a screwdriver or a bloody mary, or a whiskey sour. Something strong."

Did she say whiskey? I wasn't sure I had heard right.

"You did say whiskey didn't you?"

"Yes."

"Do you like whiskey?"

"Very much, don't you?"

I just stared straight ahead.

"Waiter, waiter...please bring me a coke, and for this young lady..."

"I'll have two drinks please...a screw driver and a whiskey sour with a wedge of lemon and lime, thank you."

My raised eyebrows and creased forehead quickly reversed into a normal expression.

The waiter brought the drinks. She raised the first glass to her lips and finished its contents in thirty seconds flat.

"You liked it?"

"Delicious. Now let me taste this one here."

She raised the second glass and knocked that one flat too.

"That was good."

I just stared into oblivion, sipping my geriatrical iced coca cola.

"The drinks helped me to unwind and relax. I'm less nervous now."

"I'm glad. You shouldn't at all let the fact that you are divorced effect your composure. Hashem decides who deserves what, and not people. He dispenses everything according to one's deeds. If you take great care in adhering to the precepts of the Torah, His ultimate wish and what He most expects from us, then you should be able to walk around with a smile on your face and a happy heart. Trust in Him. He is never unjust. He's perfect in every way. It's people who hurt, who pain, who embarrass, who cannot subdue their evil inclinations, or, who just don't care to even try. Stay away from those. You don't need them. Search out true friends. Companions who are full of *Yiras Shomayim* and *Ahavas Torah V'Chesed*. But most important of all, you must believe that what I am saying is true, for if not, then my words will have been wasted."

"I'm trying to see your point. You're so right."

But something was telling me she was just saying it. She needed a long way to go. You know, the type who are brought up frum, have Torah education shoved down their throat, go through the motions, and want to be "good Jews."

Our meeting had come to a close and I had found myself in an awkward predicament. There was no *shadchen*, a go between, to relate my decision to. Her relative was away in America. I wouldn't be able to look her in the face and tell her.

"Well I really had a meaningful time. I..."

"Aren't you going to walk me to my apartment."

We reached her building...

"I would like to tell you..."

"Come upstairs. I'll make you a tea."

"Upstairs? No, I couldn't. It's not proper."

"You must be thirsty from the walk."

"No. Really, I'm not. I'm just fine. It's getting late."

"Please! Please come upstairs. Just for tea."

"It's almost one o'clock in the morning. We'll wake your relatives."

"My cousins don't mind at all. In fact, they insisted that I bring you up to have something to eat and drink."

I felt pretty uneasy and very strange about all of this. The heaviest weight on my conscience was how to tell her. She procrastinated on making the tea; she was drawing it out.

"Thanks for the tea and everything...it's almost two, very late..."

How could I tell her?

"I would like to explain to you something. You see, I like you very much. I had a wonderful time tonight..."

"But..."

"Can you give me a couple of days to think, and I will definitely call you."

"You'll call me?"

"Yes."

"You mean it? You're not just saying it?"

"I said that I will definitely call you, and I will."

She kept me there another half hour, and if I wouldn't have put a stop to it, I might have been kept there till morning.

"It's been a pleasant evening. Thank you very much. I'll call you."

"Don't forget."

"I won't forget. Good night."

"Good night, and hoping to hear from you soon."
"Bye."
"Bye and get home safely."

As I was walking home, I began contemplating, 'What would I tell her on the phone?' How would I go about it?

Several days later a friend of mine gave me a note with a phone number on it. He said, "Call this lady Mrs. Miller. She says she has a special *shidduch* for you. Please call her this evening."

I called.

"This is Mordechai Reich."

"Yes, yes. I'm glad you called. You see, she is here with her parents from Belgium, for a two week vacation. She's a very, very special girl..."

She was a very bright girl. Sharp, intelligent, spoke seven languages fluently, and exceptionally mature for her age.

At the conclusion of the date, I couldn't be certain whether it was the right thing to meet her again. Was she really my type? After all, the Belgians were a particular type, everybody knew that. Didn't I? But she was different, something really special. A vessel that could absorb an enormous amount of knowledge. And very presentable with a bright smile and a kind face.

I called the *shadchanis* and she felt that it would be beneficial for both sides to meet again, and a time was set.

I called for her at the same address. At the conclusion of our meeting, I gathered up strength and courage and asked her if a third date would be in order. She smiled and nodded. This would be the first time that I would be seeing a girl for the third time!

I began my walk back to my apartment. Under the stars of the midnight sky, the hour and a half walk allowed me to really think everything over. I really felt that this was the one. Something was telling me that Hashem had chosen this one.

The third date, was particularly strange in nature. Before taking her to the Hilton, I had the opportunity of speaking with her parents a bit longer than usual. Sustenance, making a living, supporting their daughter, that's all they talked about...

"You want to learn? What about *parnasah*?"

"I've had experience in *chinuch* several years. If need be, I can always go back to it."

"But it makes very little. It is surely not enough. Why don't you do what my father used to do? He would get up at four in the morning, learn for an hour and go to work a whole day. Can't you do that?"

I felt it coming. Would she respond likewise? We would see. We proceeded to the Jerusalem Hilton, and sat down in one of the lounges. I began the conversation as usual with *divrey Torah, hashkafah*, and current events, weaving a tapestry. She was always keenly interested. But this time it was a bit different. She stopped me after a short while and said...

"But after everything is said and done, what about a living?"

"What do you mean?"

"It takes money to support a family."

"Therefore?"

"Well..."

"Say it out straight; Go ahead."

"What I mean to say is, what will you do for a living? How do you plan to support a family?"

She came in with the final punch. Her father had worked on her no doubt.

"Well, I was in chinuch several years. Even a principal of an entire department for two years. I can always go back to it. I love education."

"But does it pay enough? I've heard from many of my friends, who have married, kollel boys, and *melamdim*, that they are struggling very hard."

She didn't seem to be saying this from herself. Her father had done a very good job of scaring her, I could see that.

At the conclusion of the meeting, I gently and very carefully asked her if she wanted to continue. She replied in the affirmative and we arranged the fourth date for Thursday night at eight-thirty.

She wanted to see me again in spite of the 'making a living' issue. She was a Belgian girl, coming from an atmosphere where money, honor and competition rise far above the spiritual ideals of the Torah. Yet she responded and energetically so, to the Torah ideals all through our in depth conversations. She left no stone unturned. Her questions were precise and to the point. She inserted several meanings in a mere sentence. Outstandingly brilliant.

It was a very long time in coming. And what's more, her features, her warm smile, her vivaciousness and youth; the sparkle in her eye, all captivated my emotional senses.

Well, time would tell whether or not the present circumstances would materialize or dissipate into thin air. Once again, I walked the hour and a half under the stars of the night sky in thought and contemplation.

On Wednesday afternoon, the day before our scheduled date, her father appeared at my yeshiva. What did he want? Was something amiss?

I stood up as our eyes met and we approached each other, our outstretched hands grasping one another heartily.

"Shalom Aleichem, Mordechai Menachem."

"Shalom. I'm sure surprised to see you here. Is something the matter?"

"Let's talk outside. Somewhere where it's private."

We walked into the garden square.

"Mordechai, you know I admire you. You are a fine intelligent boy. But I must clear up one point though before we go any further."

Oh oh, here it comes.

"You see, my daughter is used to having the finer things in life. Our standard of living in Belgium, is quite high."

"What are you trying to say?"

"Let me get right to the point. You say you want to continue learning for a period of time, here in Israel. Now that's just fine with me. But what about *parnasah*? You mentioned that you would go back to *chinuch*. Now you and I know very well, that *chinuch* pays peanuts. You could never support my daughter. But I have an idea. What do you say to this suggestion. You could learn for a year or two, here in Israel, and I would help you out considerably: furniture, an apartment, practically whatever you need to help you along."

"And?"

"And after that you would come to Belgium and I would get you into the Diamond brokerage field. I have many contacts."

"But what about my learning?"

"Isn't two years enough? In Antwerp, two years, full time learning is very nice. After that everyone goes to work."

"But learning is my life breath. Believe me, I have tasted many occupations. This is my life blood."

"Be realistic Mordechai. Don't float in the clouds. Place your feet back down on the ground."

"But I am being realistic. Thousands of kollel *yungelite* support their families, and Boruch Hashem they are very realistic and happy in what they are doing."

"I really think that you should think things over."

"But I am clear in my aspirations. Believe me, I don't have any desire in working with diamonds, no offense. The Torah is the best diamond."

"You are not being realistic. I cannot understand you Torah boys. In Europe everybody worked. Now, there is a new style, to sit and learn a whole day. It is not for my daughter. She needs expensive things. This is the way it is in Antwerp."

"Yes."

"Allright, I've tried to convince you to be reasonable, but I see that you are staunch in your ways."

"What are you driving at?"

"Let me get down to the point. After the third date, I decided to break off the whole thing. It was clear that your way of life, was not for my daughter. But I said to myself, no, there could still be a chance. If you would agree, to come to Belgium and work in diamonds, things could be worked out. But now I see that I'm wrong."

"What do you mean to bring out by all of this?"

"Well, I'm sorry to have to tell you this, but I cannot allow you to see my daughter, again, unless, you promise that you will agree to my condition."

It hit me like an express train, knocking the wind out of me. It took me at least thirty seconds to digest his statement.

"Is this Sarah's decision?"

"It is my decision."

"But can't she decide for herself, what she wants in life? She's a very capable girl."

"I'm her father. I know what's best for her."

"But my question is, if this decision was hers. You see the reason I'm asking you this is because, from the meetings we had together, she conveyed a very strong desire, to join me in this Torah way of life."

"That is why I stepped in now."

"In other words, the decision to discontinue, is yours alone."

"What is the difference? I am her father!"

We weren't going to get anywhere this way, that was for sure. I had to think of a plan...

"Mr. Richman let me suggest something, if I may. Sarah and I made up to meet tomorrow evening, is that right?"

"That's correct."

"Now, if she decides to discontinue after our date, it will be final, and I will accept it."

"No, I cannot allow that."

"But what is there to be afraid of?"

"It is out of the question. Unless you agree to my condition you shall not see her again."

"Now, Mr. Richman, let's look at it this way. A man of his word, must keep it. Wasn't I promised a fourth date?"

"By her, not by me."

"Oh I see."

He had an iron grip on her. Daddy's girl, or was she just afraid of him?

"Mr. Reich, I give you one last chance to accept my condition."

"I'm sorry, truly sorry. You want me to be what I am not. If I would promise to go to Belgium, I would just be lying to myself."

"Then your final answer is no?"

"No to your condition. Not no to your daughter."

"You are very stubborn, Mordechai, very, very stubborn."

"For Hashem and His Torah, I am proud not to budge."

"Well then it is settled. It is off. I'm truly sorry, you decided it this way."

I had dreams and aspirations. Things were going so well, and then someone comes along and takes it all away, snap just like that. A father who doesn't allow his daughter to decide for herself, a man who thinks that because he is much older and experienced, that he cannot listen to someone younger than him, to listen and to listen well, in the hope that he might learn something new, something he didn't know before.

"I tried my best. You don't want to accept my condition at all, not even with a modification."

"But don't you see? I'm not trying to be stubborn, believe me. I just can't go against the grain of my aspirations. Can't you understand? I'm not doing it to show anybody that I'm tough."

Seeing that I was most sincere in my words, he said...

"Mordechai, there was something I kept hidden from you, and now I must tell you. Sarah is not for you. She has a mongoloid brother," and he waited for my response.

"So what?"

"So what!!!"

He didn't believe what he had heard me just say.

"You don't care? It doesn't bother you?"

"Of course not! What should that have to do with Sarah? Do you think that Hashem Yisborach, denies a person his or her *zivug* because of that? Mr. Richman, I'm surprised at you!"

"Do you mean that?"

"To the fullest."

I'm shocked at your reply. You are the first boy that she has met, that wanted to continue on, even after finding out about it. I have the greatest of respect for you."

"Then..."

"But, Mordechai, I still must keep things in their proper perspective. Sarah is my daughter. I am worried for her. I want the best for her. Can't you understand? Of course you can't. You don't know what it is to be a father, spending sleepless nights, worrying sick about his daughter, till she finds the right boy."

"But where's your *bitachon*? Trust in Hashem!"

"Hashem wants you to work and make a living too. He doesn't throw down bread from the sky. I just cannot let you see her again, without agreeing to my condition."

Again, we were going in circles. We weren't getting anywhere. It seemed rather apparent, that he was quite afraid of letting me see his daughter even just once more. Maybe he didn't recognize her anymore, since she had met me. She was in a new world, a frightening Torah oriented atmosphere. "What has this boy done to my daughter?" I'm sure was going repeatedly through his mind. "She always listened to my advice, and now all of a sudden this boy has changed her opinions and ideas. She wants a kollel boy! I must put a stop to this right away, before it gets out of hand, before he completely has her in his power!"

Mrs. Miller had mentioned during one of our phone conversations that she was indeed astonished, to learn that Sarah still wanted to see me, after the first date, even after I had expressed my intentions of Torah study and *chinuch*.

"You know Mordechai," she said, "To tell you the truth, I was sure that Sarah would not agree to see you again after the first date."

"Why not?"

"Well because, she's not looking for a kollel boy! Never was!"

"Then why did you suggest her to me? Didn't you know that I was set on learning?"

"I wasn't aware of that. I thought you would learn for a year, and then go to work."

"Didn't R. Waldman inform you?"

"No, not to that extent. But you must have said something or done something special, because she wanted to see you again..."

In other words, her father had noticed and was aware of that same change in her...he was frightened. I could clearly tell.

"Can I at least call her?"

"You are not to call her. Is that understood?"

"I see."

"Besides, she is seeing another boy tonight."

This was some kind of trick, up his sleeve, no doubt, to get me disinterested in the whole situation.

"She's seeing someone else tonight?"

"Mr. Reich, it is settled. There is nothing further to discuss. Good day."

That evening, I called Mrs. Miller.

"You heard I'm sure."

"Yes, indeed."

"Tell me Mrs. Miller. Is it true. Is she seeing another boy tonight?"

"No! Of course not."

"I thought so."

I made another phone call...

"Hello Mr. Richman?"

"Yes, who's this?"

"Mordechai."

"Yes, what is it."

"I've just gotten off the phone with Mrs. Miller, and she explicitly said that Sarah is not seeing another boy tonight."

"I'm going to call her!" and he hung up.

Two minutes later, I got a phone call.

"Mordechai?"

"Yes, – Mrs. Miller?"

"Yes, – My goodness. What did you do? He just called and gave it to me over the head!"

"But why?"

"She is seeing a boy tonight."

"What?!!"

"I didn't tell you, because I didn't want to hurt your feelings. You've had enough for one day."

"But I don't quite understand. You said that she was crazy about me. Why then would she be seeing another boy tonight?"

"Yes it's true, she was wild over you and she still very much is, I guarantee you that. But you see, this boy's parents have been after Sarah for a long time now, pestering her parents to no end. As Sarah is leaving to Belgium soon — by the way she'll stay on, if you accept her father's condition — these people have coaxed Mr. and Mrs. Richman to agree upon the meeting of their children. And so, even though Sarah is completely disinterested in the boy, she has no other choice but to see him and get him out of the way. You know how people talk."

"I see. Mr. Richman must have been quite upset."

"Quite."

"What do you suggest be done now? Do you have any advice? I seem to be in a daze."

"Listen, Mordechai. She's wild about you. Let me tell you, something her cousin told me, after you had seen her for the second time: She said, "You know Mrs. Miller, I've never seen Sarah so nervous. It's that boy. He's sure affecting her emotions. She even cut our visit short, remarking, 'I have to go now, I'm seeing him tonight; it's already four o'clock! My hair's a mess, just a mess. Which dress should I wear? The expensive one? My I must go now, I must be ready...' So you see Mordechai, I'm sure the father is pulling all the levers..."

"So what do you suggest?"

"Mordechai, listen to me. There's only one thing for you to say and everything will continue on normally. Say that you are willing to go to Belgium after one or two years of kollel. Give me the word, and I'll call Mr. Richman, and you'll see her tomorrow."

"Mrs. Miller, I can't. I want to but I just can't. I went through all this with Sarah's father. He doesn't understand. What I would like to know is if, this is Sarah's decision. I mean, is she also frightened about, *parnasah*?"

"Mordechai, let me be frank with you. I come from Belgium. They eat meat every night. They live expensively. They travel by jet, at least once a year, to their parents, from where ever they are in the world. Can you afford to give her all these things, on a kollel salary?"

She said it so naturally, and so matter-of-factly, that I started feeling: Maybe I am not cut out for this situation after all.

"Mordechai, I was in Belgium. Now that I'm in Eretz Yisroel, things are much different. We have a simpler way of life in general. But if Sarah's father distinctly wants you to come and settle in Belgium, the only way to do that is by getting a good salary, as all the others have, who live there."

"But what does Sarah say?"

"I tried to speak to her. Her father did not let me. So you see, it is her father who's in charge. Just give me the word and I'll call him."

"I can't. I just can't."

"Think it over, but not for too long. They're leaving this Sunday to Belgium."

She continued, "Sarah has a cousin, Mr. Richman's nephew, who owns an optical shop in the city. This is his address. His name is Mr. Kopel. Speak with him. Try to find out, what Sarah's opinion is. He's very close with her."

"Thanks alot, that's a very good idea," and I said goodnight.

As I hung up, I began thinking things over. I even spoke with a number of qualified and authoritative experts on the subject, whether or not to agree to Mr. Richman's condition, and if it was within the guidelines of the Torah. Friends advised, "You're silly! Promise him the world, marry her, and good bye. After two years in Israel, she'll be so attached to you that you'll have her in the bag. You've got it made!" "Oh no," I replied, "I'm not promising anything I have no intention of doing."

I spoke with Mr. Kopel in his shop that Friday morning for quite some time.

"Look here," he said. "See your phone number on this telephone book? It's been there over a month. Sarah's father was checking up on you for already a month and a half. He made dozens of phone calls from Belgium to Israel to find out as much information about you as possible. He was impressed with the references and was waiting anxiously for Mrs. Miller to set up a date between you and Sarah. You were in the Galil for about a week. Mrs. Miller couldn't get a hold of you."

"My, you've been practically following me."

"Let me tell you something. If you would only know how many phone calls Mr. Richman made to me about you this past week!"

"He confides in you."

"He knows, Sarah is very dear to me. He is confident that I would do only the best for her."

We talked about things in general; about learning, working, the Yeshiva boy of today, his boyhood history and how he wished he could have remained in yeshiva. Then he came in with the pitch...

"It's a shame that you are not willing to agree to Mr. Richman's terms. You're losing an outstanding girl, believe me. I know her like a brother. You're letting your *zivug* slip right through your fingers."

"Mr. Kopel, can you readily swear that Mr. Richman's terms and Sarah, are both preordained from Heaven. Are you one thousand percent certain and sure of it?"

"Well..."

"Can you attest, that this is what Hashem is expecting of me; namely to abandon a life of Torah study for Mr. Richman's conditions?"

"I can't, but..."

"Let's see how it falls. Let's be patient."

He was impressed with my analysis and confided to me that Mr. and Mrs. Richman and Sarah would be spending Shabbos with him and his family and that he would call me if there were any changes in the developments.

Saturday night passed and it was Sunday morning. They would be leaving for Belgium in the evening. I dialed Mrs. Miller...She picked up.

"It's you Mordechai, isn't it."

"How did you know?"

"My husband said you would definitely call. As a matter of fact, as the phone rang he remarked that it was you."

"Mrs. Miller, I spoke with Mr. Kopel and we had a long discussion. He concluded that he would call me in the event there were new developments."

"I know. I spoke with him today."

"Did he tell you about our conversation?"

"Yes, indeed."

"Did he relate anything in particular?"

"He said, that they spoke about you at the table."

"Excuse me for interrupting, but who's they?"

"The Richman family. Well actually the Mrs. and Sarah and everyone else, except Mr. Richman."

"I see. And..."

"They voiced their desire to discuss the situation, especially Sarah and her mother, but Mr. Richman said the story's over, and there's nothing more to talk about, and that's that. He didn't want to hear about it anymore. Five minutes later, they started in again regarding you. Poor Sarah. Mr. Richman reiterated, that the case was closed, and that was his final decision. A lot that helped him, because Sarah and her mother just kept on bringing it up again and again. She still wants you Mordechai, and very badly. Her father has her in his iron hold. What should she do?"

"I understand. She hasn't the strength to disobey her father's wishes."

"Sarah kept on nudging her father, and so much so, that he began thinking about you in the positive sense again. He calmed Sarah by promising her, that he would see into the whole thing, later on, when he would travel to New York, your hometown, on diamond business, and that he would check up on you in greater detail. He's a bit scared Mordechai, to tell you the truth. He likes you but, he's not sure if your ideals are built on a solid rock foundation. He's afraid that you are one of those unrealistic idealists. He said that if he likes what he hears, then he will send Sarah to Israel, to see you, all by herself. He'll be going to New York in about a month."

"It sounds like water under the bridge."

"Mordechai, I think he really means it."

"Oh well. It seemed like it was so close. Yet now, all I have are words and ifs. Mrs. Miller, I would like to thank you kindly for all your help, really. You've been so nice to me."

"Don't mention it."

"Shalom and thank you again."

"Shalom and feel good. Don't let this get you down. Everything will turn out fine."

As I hung up the phone, a cold hand gripped my heart. Only once before had this happened to me. In the years of dating, this was only the second such experience. Very bitter. Very depressing.

I must pinpoint the cause of my emotional distress, I told myself. What had I done, to disturb someone else's emotions.? Yes...Yes, of course. I had promised to call her! That's it. How could I have done this to her. True, it was difficult for me, and I was pushing it off, because I didn't know how to say what I wanted to say. How I wished there was a *shadchan* to go between us, yes all of this was very true, however, that did not vindicate me, in any way whatsoever, to procrastinate and push off that phone call. I felt just terrible.

Quickly, I searched for her number and nervously dialed. I began sweating profusely...

"Hello."

"Yes! Mordechai?"

"Yes, it's me."

"It's good to hear your voice. You finally called. You kept your word. I was waiting and waiting, and then I just gave up. I was sure you had dropped me."

"I'm so sorry, but I went through a very traumatic experience this past week, and I needed a clear head to think things through. I'm sorry, really sorry. Do you forgive me?"

"Of course."

And then silence. Stark silence. Hashem help me. Please, help me say the right words. Don't let her get hurt more. It's enough of hurting going around for one day.

"Are you there?"

"Yes..."

I began very gently. I think she knew it was coming. I spoke with her for about thirty minutes. We talked things out. She was disappointed, I felt that. Yet she showed me she was prepared for it. She remarked that even if it wasn't meant to be, she would always remember the kindness and thoughtfulness, I showed her. The *hashkafa* and enlightening words of Torah that I shared with her. She mentioned that I had taught her a new and different approach, a distinctive optimistic outlook in life, which would equip her to stabilize her checks and balances, and would afford her to stand strong and feel a deep sense of self worth, through the difficult tribulations ahead.

We concluded our conversation, with mutual blessings of success in finding our true *zivugim*.

That night it was difficult to fall asleep. I tossed and turned till the morning light and then I fell into a deep slumber. When I awoke, I began contemplating about something that had entered my mind during the course of my short acquaintance with Miss. Richman. Sarah's address in Yerushalayim during her brief stay was Rechov Uziel 91.

Two interesting items: I had just been to Amukah which was associated with the name Uziel and the numerical value 91 formed the Hebrew letters *tzadi aleph* and ultimately the word *tzei* which meant "Go", or to "Go out" as regards to dating. It seemed unrealistic and far from concrete to go on, yet somehow I might have found it quite interesting and therefore placed a bit too much seriousness and hope into it, and I hurt all the more for it.

Two weeks had gone by and I was just then beginning to adjust. I had developed a serious cough, which would not go away. My younger brother suggested that if I were to hope of getting better, I would be wise in returning to America where experts in medical care would attend to my illness. "Besides," he added, "Mother mentioned that she would very much like that you come back."

I thought to myself, I've been here about a year, have seen so many prospects and still no results. Maybe it was about time to return to America and see how prospects would turn out there. *Meshaneh makon meshaneh mazal.*

Having decided upon doing that after several days of intensive deliberation, I called Mrs. Miller to tell her about my plans.

"Hello, this is Mordechai Reich."

"Hello."

"I'm calling to let you know that I'm planning to go to America sometime within the next couple of weeks and I do not know for sure yet whether I'll be coming back. If Mr. Richman decides to contact me I'll be in New York, well, actually in Lakewood."

"I'm so sorry; I have another girl from Antwerp, a very rich one, who wants very much to meet you around Succos time."

"Rich? That's not my criteria. Torah ideals, remember?"

"Yes, yes. But money always helps. And don't forget, you want to learn. You need money for that. This girl's father by the way is loaded and want's a learning boy. Their name is Wise."

"What can I say? I have a terrible cough which just won't go away and my mother is adamant that I come back to America. It's been about a year since she's seen me."

"I understand. Allright, you go on to America and if anything develops I'll send the Wise girl to New York."

"What?"

"Her father sends her to New York as frequently as we take buses. He's really loaded."

"Well, whatever happens, let me thank you for all that you have done for me and may you have success in all your endeavors."

"Thank you very much. May you find your *zivug b'meherah* and never experience any more pain."

"Thank you. Shalom."

"Shalom *v'kol tuv*."

As I hung the phone it occurred to me that the issue was far from over.

Chapter Fourteen

Trans-Atlantic Search

My jet touched down at Kennedy International Airport. I was back in New York. I wondered what lay ahead.

I was nursed back to health under a specialist's care. Succos passed and I returned to the Lakewood Yeshiva. Several weeks later when I was home for a Shabbos weekend, my friend Sheya Mendlowitz informed me that his friend had related to him that he had spoken with a Mr. Richman, who had asked many questions about me. Sarah's father was in New York! It wasn't a made up story after all. He was checking up on me.

On a Sunday afternoon, about a week later, the phone rang in my home. I was home at the time attending to *shiduchim* matters, and so I was present when that mysterious phone call arrived. Mother picked up.

"Hello, who is this? You say your name is Mr. Rosenberg and you are here with a friend. And you want to see me this evening. Well what exactly is the purpose of the visit? You say it's a private matter, not to be discussed over the phone. I see. Yes, I understand. Not to breathe a word of it to my son who is learning presently in Lakewood. Well I understand to some extent, but you'll have to clarify your intentions..."

It must be him. But who was he with and why was he disguising his identity?

"Fine, I'll be expecting you at about eight this evening. Goodbye," and she hung up.

"Who was it? Mr. Richman, I gather."

"A Mr. Rosenberg with a friend. You heard."

"Well, I can find out. I'll be in the back room."

"No, no. I can't let you do that. They made me promise that you would not be around when they came. Otherwise, they reiterated, they would not come. My word is my word."

"Allright, I'll be out of the house before they arrive."

At about seven-thirty, I put my hat and jacket on and left for Yeshiva Torah Vodass. I *davened* maariv with great fervor requesting spiritual guidance through this sudden turn of events. Nine thirty I returned home.

"They were Belgian, no doubt," my mother said.

"What were their names."

"Mr. Rosenberg and Mr. Wise."

"What did they talk about?"

"First they began talking amongst themselves in Hungarian, while I was preparing coffee in the kitchen. They thought I didn't understand Hungarian and so they spoke freely. After their many compliments about our beautiful home, one of them turned to me and started asking detailed questions about you."

"What did he want to know?"

He asked, "Does your boy really want to learn? Is he realistic about his ideals? What will he do about *parnasah*?"

"What did you reply?"

"That you were definitely quite serious about continuing in learning and that you would handle the *parnasah*."

"Anything else?"

"Oh yes. One of them mentioned that he heard that you were quite staunch and unyielding in your ways, and 'why doesn't he come down from the clouds.'"

"That's Mr. Richman, I just know it is."

"They said their names were Mr. Rosenberg and Mr. Wise."

"But that's just how Mr. Richman talked in Yerushalayim. Those same remarks. On second thought, Mrs. Miller did mention the Wise girl from Belguim...could it be that one of them was actually Mr. Wise?"

"You see, you can never tell. Maybe Mrs. Miller spoke with Mr. Wise, giving him Mr. Richman for references. He had in turn spoken with Mr. Richman extensively about you, and that's how he knew to ask those same questions."

"I don't know what to think."

"Well, I guess whatever their intentions were, we'll either soon know about them, or not know about them at all."

Several days later, I decided that I would once and for all clear the air and attempt to find out what was actually going on, by writing an indepth letter to Miss. Richman. It took much courage and stamina, and a great deal of searching for her proper address, but it was accomplished.

I wrote: Dear Sarah, I hope that you are well. I am writing in essence because my conscience dictates me to. There is one thing that I must clear up. And that is to know your considerations and feelings regarding us. Was the decision to discontinue, your father's alone, or yours also? Please clarify in a letter. It would help me to solve and finalize, a seemingly never ending thought which lingers constantly in the back of my mind.

Please feel free to write your exact feelings on the issue. I will understand either way.

* * *

Three weeks passed without incident, and then in Lakewood...

"Mordechai Menachem, someone called earlier today to speak with you."

"Yes?"

"All the way from Belgium."

"From Belgium!?"

I took hold of myself.

"From Antwerp Belgium. He said that he wanted to speak with Mordechai Reich and Mordechai Reich only."

"What was his name? What was the purpose of his call?"

"He didn't say. But what he did say was that he would call again in the afternoon, and he asked me to request of you, to be near the phone, when he calls."

"I wonder who it could be. From Belgium?"

"My, my, *shadchanim* are out for you, all the way from Europe. Imagine that!"

Actually I was hoping...yet retaining a realistic attitude. I waited for the phone call impatiently, and in the afternoon it came through.

"Hello."

"Hello. I wish to speak with Mordechai Reich, please. This is long distance from Belgium."

"This is he."

"Ah good! Mr. Reich, I would like to speak with you, concerning a *shidduch*."

"Yes, go ahead."

"You see, let me get down to the point. I have spoken extensively with Mrs. Miller..."

"Yes..."

"You know her..."

"Yes of course. A very nice lady."

"Indeed. A fine woman. Well, we spoke about you concerning a girl from Belgium."

My apprehension and anxiety were intensifying with each passing second. Was he going to say...

"Her name is Miss Wise."

My heart sank.

I regained my composure.

"A Miss Wise. Yes...yes. Mrs. Miller did mention her to me while I was in Yerushalayim."

"Now Mr. Reich, I know that her father wants his daughter to meet with you, and Mr. Reich, this is between you and me, he wants this meeting very much so."

"Does she want a learning boy?"

"Yes."

"Does her father want the same?"

"Very much so."

"I see. Well, what about the actual meeting? I mean, I'm here in Lakewood, and she's in Belgium."

"That's no problem. No problem at all. She can come to New York in a couple of days."

"A couple of days?"

"Yes. Her father is waiting for your reply. Now remember, if you do not want to see her, then you must tell me so now. She will only accompany her father on his diamond business trip, if you clearly state that you will see her when she arrives in New York."

"You know, I feel rather awkward. She'll be traveling across the ocean, just to see me, and that would put me in a strange position indeed."

"Nothing to be alarmed about. She comes to New York, many times a year."

"Really."

"Of course. There are many more prospects here than there are in Antwerp. Do you understand now?"

"I think I do. Let me just think for a few seconds, to clear my thoughts...Allright, I will agree to meet with her."

"Very good. Now, Mr. Wise will be arriving in New York this Thursday. He will be staying at the Park House Hotel. Naturally his daughter will be with him, as per our conversation. Please call him at his hotel, Thursday evening, and you'll take it from there. Now one more thing. If you decide to continue with her, please call me collect. Here is my number."

"Thank you and I will keep in touch."

"Very well. I will say goodbye now and good luck."

"Thank you very much. Good bye."

From Belgium. All the way from Europe. A definite first for me. But couldn't the phone call have been about 'her'? The thought of it caused me a bit of uneasiness and sadness.

Thursday arrived, I traveled to Brooklyn, and in the evening I called. It was set for Sunday evening. At the Park House, Sunday evening, Mr. Wise and I conversed thirty minutes or so. Then his daughter appeared. After our meeting we said a proper good night and departed. The typical Belgian. It was over even before it had started.

Monday afternoon back in Lakewood, I dialed Antwerp, Belgium...

"Yes, hello. This is Mordechai Reich, from America."

"Yes, Mordechai. How was it? You wish to continue I suppose."

"Well, she's a very nice person, but just not for me."

"Oh I see...I really wished you wouldn't have called. I distinctly told you that if you decided to continue, you should call me. Now that you tell me you are not interested, you should have left it at that; not to call me to notify me you are rejecting her. It's quite degrading you know. In Antwerp, if a girl hears no response from the boy after several days, she knows that he is not interested."

"I understand. But my responsibility and conscience, directed me to call. I just can't let a person, especially a young girl, hang in mid-air. I did it once, and paid very dearly for it."

"Well, I think it's best, that I don't tell her anything. I'll leave it the way it is. Besides it's easier for me not to have to say to her father, a very rich and influential member of the community, that someone did not want his daughter."

"I guess you have to do what you have to do. Before I say goodbye, may I ask of you a favor?"

"Yes, what is it."

"Do you know the Richman family, specifically Sarah?"

"Yes I do. Why do you ask?"

"Well, I wrote her a letter, a very important one about three weeks ago, and I just want to make sure that she received it. Can you do me a special favor, and tell her that I sent it to her, registered? This way, if in the event she did not receive it, she will at least know that a letter was to have been coming to her."

"I shall be glad to do that for you, Mordechai."

"Thank you very kindly. And thank you for your efforts and considerations on my behalf."

"You are most definitely welcome. Mordechai, may you find your *zivug* soon."

"Amen, and thank you again. Goodbye."

"Goodbye."

Approximately two weeks later Sarah's letter arrived. My hands held the letter with as much care, as one would exercise holding an expensive crystal vase. She replied. She was considerate. Slowly and carefully, I opened the envelope, and began to read. She had written in English, one of her seven fluent languages:

Dear Mordechai, I received your letter but found it very difficult deciding how to start my letter to you. How could I express the proper words with which to portray my feelings about us?

First I want to say that it wasn't totally my father's decision to discontinue. You see, Mordechai, originally I never even dreamt of wanting to meet a Kollel boy. It just wasn't for me. The way of life would be much too hard for me. I'm used to having the things I want. But then when I met you, something changed in me. I started feeling and understanding your way of life. That it had purpose and ideals. Your *divrei Torah* were very enlightening and inspiring. I felt it during our dates. But after each date, when I came home, I realized that I lacked your foundation, your beliefs. "Could I really endure such a life of hardship? Am I idealistic like Mordechai? I'm afraid not." I kept on convincing myself.

Mordechai, I am not on your high level. You deserve a girl who is ready for your Torah and *mesiras nefesh* way of life. You'll find her soon. I give you a *bracha* that you will meet your proper *zivug b'meheirah*. I know that you will understand me and that our mutual hurt will heal with the passing of time.

I read and reread the letter. I extracted every possible nuance, every slight innuendo, every subtle hint. I was certain that her father had succeeded in convincing her that my way of life was absolutely not for her.

There was no doubt in my mind that if her father were to give his blessings to our union, that we would have been engaged in Yerushalayim, months ago. He, no doubt, made her wary of the dangerous prospect of getting married to a man who could surely not raise the proper amount of funds to sustain a family.

I folded the letter and placed it in my shirt pocket. She had replied. It showed me that she was conscientious. I would acknowledge receipt of her letter, which would either conclude our relationship, owing to the contents therein, or if she so desired, if for some reason she would feel that it would be beneficial to continue a correspondence for the purpose of thinking things over seriously, then she would have the perogative of doing so. Actually, I wasn't too certain if a letter to her from me now, was the proper thing to do, since her letter might have been a signal hinting that this was the final conclusion. I would have to think it over.

I called my mother that evening...

"Hi. Guess what? I received a letter from Sarah today."

"What did she write? What has she to say?"

"In essence she explained that it wasn't only her father's decision. She expressed that she herself did not feel she was ready to settle down with a kollel boy. And so on. But she was very nice about it all. I give her credit. She handled it properly."

"Now I can tell you."

"What?"

"You know those two men who visited me, Mr. Wise and Mr. Rosenberg?"

"Yes."

"Well it was Mr. Richman and another man."

"How do you know?"

"Because the day after their visit I met the other man on the street and he said to me that if I would give him my word not to tell you who the man with him was, he would tell me. I agreed to his condition and he said it was Mr. Richman! Now that you've received a letter from her, concluding the chapter, I felt I could tell you that secret."

"I knew it! I knew he was one of the men! The way he spoke with you in the house gave him away."

He hadn't changed his course of action or questioning. He remained loyally steadfast to his standard and criteria. He was protecting his daughter. I had to give him credit for that.

"There will be other fine prospects. Keep up your learning and before you know it, the right one will come along."

"I'm sure. Thanks Ma. I would like to ask you, do you think writing a letter acknowledging that I received hers, is such a good idea?"

"It won't hurt. But explain that you fully understand her decision and that you accept it as final, unless she would like to think about it otherwise. It's allright. Just make sure your words are clear, concise and unambiguous. And yes don't forget. Be very gentle. Girls are very sensitive you know."

"Yes. I know. Well, thanks Ma for your advice. Take care."

"Everything will be allright, don't you worry."

"Bye."

"Bye, and learn well."

As I hung up the phone I began contemplating: Should I write that letter or not? What would I say? Would it come across right? Or would I just be making matters worse. Should I leave things as they were and accept that her letter was a clear indication of the finalization on the issue? Or was she actually waiting for some reply, some thread of hope, which would give her an excuse to give some serious thought and realistic consideration about us.

After several days of intensive deliberation, I decided to write it. I sat down and worked hard at it; two hours and many crumpled pages. Finally it was finished. I folded the letter and placed it at the upper right corner of my desk. It stayed there for about a week. I still couldn't decide whether or not to send it.

The next day, when I was in a *seforim* store, I noticed a display stand containing key chains over by the counter. Personal Hebrew first names were engraved upon the colorful acrylic round shaped key chains and all of them were bunched together except for two, which were distinctly separate and by themselves: Menachem and Sarah. Menachem was on top, and Sarah was directly below.

I posted the letter the next morning.

About a week later, in the yeshiva study hall...

"Mordechai Menachem, my close friend from Yeshivas Chevron

just got engaged yesterday. He's going to leave Yeshiva and settle in Antwerp, where he'll be working in diamonds."

"I guess the girl's from Belgium."

"Yes. From Antwerp."

I placed my *sefer* down as I looked into my friend's eyes and asked, "Do you by any chance know her name?"

"Let me think. Let me see if I can remember. Yes, her name is...Richman...Sarah Richman."

My eyes looked away and down at the table.

"What's wrong Mordechai? You look a bit surprised. What is it?"

"Nothing. Nothing at all."

"Did you know her?"

"Did I know her? Well...I guess you could say that I did."

Chapter Fifteen

The Lesson of Amukah

Asarah B'Teves, a day of fasting and affliction, the very day that I had learned she had gotten engaged. It was arranged so that my pain coincide with the pain and affliction of this very holy fast day.

The purpose of a fast day, the ultimate benefit to be derived from it, is the awakening of the heart to do *Teshuvah*, to promise to accept Hashem's will, and to walk in His way, through the performance of His commandments. An additional benefit accrued through fasting is the awakening of the spiritual conscience, through minimizing materialistic desires, hence the abstention from food and drink.

At the close of *Asarah B'Teves*, my thoughts and feelings continued contemplating about the whole situation. How much longer would I have to wait? How many more hearts would be broken? When would I merit my *zivug*? I knew that to get the answers to these questions, I would have to search out my ways and correct them. This was the message of *Asarah B'Teves*.

That night, I dreamt a most interesting dream: In my dream a voice said, "As Hashem is One and His Name is One, so too, there is only one special *zivug* prepared and waiting for you. You must wait for her!"

I woke up with a start - it was morning. I said 'Modeh Ani' with great fervor, *davened*, and had breakfast in the yeshiva dining room, all the while thinking about the message from the voice in my dream. After breakfast, I proceeded to the *bais hamidrash* to learn. I opened my *gemarah* to continue with my studies, and the words on the page (Megillah 30b), reawakened, the dream:

The *gemarah* spoke of the obligation of searching out one's ways and contemplating one's sins and transgressions during a fast day, in order to admit, confess, and correct them. The *gemarah* continued to say that the last quarter of the fast day should be set aside for the purpose of confession and correction. This was exactly my case. The final quarter of *Asarah B'Teves* was spent in contemplation and confession. I had begun searching and probing for the reasons of my broken heart in conjunction with the finding of my true *zivug*. Only then was I granted the startling dream.

My friends — who can even begin to try to fathom Hashem's hidden and mysterious ways? It is something like a dream. In actuality a fantasy of grand aspirations. *Rabos machashavos b'lev ish, v'atzas Hashem he sakum* - Many are man's thoughts (thinking that he definitely knows why this and this occurred), but the actuality of events is that Hashem's purpose and intention (which is hidden) stand alone to be established and fixed; only His thoughts, and not our opinions of them.

The pain associated with finding one's *zivug* is terribly immense. How much suffering I had endured despite the *davening* and tears and the indepth contemplation and inner soul-searching. I thought all the while, that I was somewhat in control of my destiny. But Hashem, through the ordeal of Amukah, clearly showed me that it was He that would determine the future according to my spiritual progress, and not me through my guesses and gropings in the dark.

The way of Hashem, our understanding of His ways and how He operates, is closed-up. Shut away; indefinite. We cannot grasp His infiniteness, His perfectness, His power! As the *Navi* in the *haftorah* of *Asarah B'Teves* proclaims: "For My thoughts are not as your thoughts, and My ways are not as your ways, declares, Hashem!"

They are hidden and closed up as it is stated: "For all hidden mysteries and things are know to Hashem (but) only those things which are revealed to us, are we and our sons to be busy with to do them." We must constantly keep in mind, that Hashem's actions are righteous, and we should accept them wholeheartedly, in spite of the fact that we do not grasp, we do not understand the inifinite wisdom, the supremacy of His justice and merciful attributes.

My friends! The way to Amukah was closed up, but in the end I succeeded in getting there. I almost despaired, almost gave up - but in the end success was mine.

And Amukah itself was situated in a hidden closed up valley, tucked away in the hidden recesses of a mystical forest.

Amukah, as we have already learned, means 'deep'. Since R. Yonoson b. Uziel knew the secret, actually the deep and closed away secret of Moshiach's exact moment of arrival, which Hashem did not want him to reveal, he was therefore destined to be buried in a secret, deep, and closed up, out of the way valley, hidden and extremely hard to get to, for the fact remains that the secret of Moshiach's exact moment of arrival still remains very deep and closed away from all of us. In this vein, Rashi commentates on Parshas VaYechi: Why is this chapter "closed up?" Because Yaakov *Avinu* wished to reveal the end of all exiles to his sons, but it was closed up from him. Hashem shut that secret away.

Yaakov *Avinu* and Yonoson b. Uziel, both wished to reveal the end of days, but it was 'closed up' from them.

The way to Amukah seemed closed, Amukah itself was situated in a closed away valley, the prospective dates were closed away from my comprehension, as was the significance to be learned by all of this - and that was that Hashem's hidden and mysterious ways, are deep and closed away from mankind's finite and simplistic intellect.

Asarah B'Teves, the proper time for the message: "My ways and thoughts are far removed from yours. What is revealed to you, you must do, but keep away from hidden and closed up things." Leave them exclusively to Me. They are "Amuk" too deep for you. I shall grant you your *zivug* in due time. Do not think that you will decide the time for Me. You may pray for guidance, as did David when he prayed: *M'mamakim k'rasicha* - "From out of the depths (Amek), do I call out to you!" I do not understand your "deep" and "closed up" ways. Guide and help me; aid me to do what is right and just in Your eyes. Help me to choose the proper one, with sincere prayer from the hidden depths of my heart!

Amukah, the hidden valley. The hidden solution to success in *Avodas Hashem*.

Chapter Sixteen

The Dream

I had the following dream on a Shabbos afternoon, Parshas Bamidbar, Erev Rosh Chodesh Sivan, the fourty-forth day of the *Sefirah*, between the hours of two-thirty and five-thirty p.m.:

Before experiencing this dream, I had prayed to Hashem to answer my prayer and send me the right *zivug*, so that I should not have to cause or experience any more pain. Then I fell asleep.

I was standing in the middle of a wide open meadow. The sun was shining, but was getting ready to set. I noticed a forest in the distance, and began walking towards it. Upon reaching the forest's edge, I noticed a small opening which offered what seemed to be a tiny entrance path leading into her dense domain. I hesitated at first to embark upon the path, as I observed that the sun was setting rather markedly. But I calculated that I would still be able to enter the forest, take a stroll on the path, and yet have ample time to return to the forest's edge before the sun's setting would bring with it total darkness.

I entered the forest's mysterious domain and almost immediately a severe degree of darkness prevailed. The numerous trees blocked most of the sunlight out, yet I could still catch an intermittent glimpse of the sun's round shape.

I continued on the path which began gradually climbing upwards. Several moments later, a forboding abyss appeared up ahead which forced my path to veer to the left.

I continued on the path, ascending with it higher and higher. On my right, not more than a mere three feet away, was the very dark and deep abyss, and the higher I got, the more frightened I became.

Clouds of mist began forming above the abyss and suddenly I felt the sense of being high above the world. Then my eye caught sight of a glorious rainbow, which had just formed above the abyss, and it was curving into the clouds of mist. I felt a tingling sensation of standing at the threshold of purpose - at the cornerstone of my life.

The darkness was growing more intense now, and I could see through the trees that the sun was setting now very rapidly. Darker and darker the forest became. I decided to turn back. I turned around very carefully and exercised extreme caution in my descent. Any slight trip would surely send me to my end.

The path was getting harder and harder to follow. If I could only reach the point where the path turned off and away from the abyss, I would be safe.

Slowly and steadily, I proceeded to descend. I shot a quick glance towards the abyss and shuddered. "*Bitachon*" I murmured to myself. "Hashem will surely guide me out of the forest."

Finally I reached the point where the path turned off and away from the abyss. I let out a sigh of relief.

I continued on the path that would eventually lead me out of the forest. But now, I could not see the path at all, as the forest was completely without any trace of light. How would I find my way to the edge?

Suddenly my eyes caught sight of a sparkle, a tiny ray of light in the distance. It must be the opening at the forest's edge, I thought. I kept my eyes on that tiny shred of light, and like a blind man, used the distant light as my cane. I proceeded very cautiously down the path, until - there it was! The exit at the forest's edge!

How relieved I felt, when I finally reached the spacious open meadow. I took deep breaths of fresh country air, and experienced the tingling sensation of being born again.

The sun now was almost completely gone. Dusk had set in. I proceeded through the meadow, towards a house which had its lights on. I entered the house, and excitedly told its inhabitants of my adventure, and of my blessed deliverance. To each one I recounted my story of Divine guidance.

I approached one of the dining tables, where I began to recount my story to an individual, whom I felt I knew from somewhere before, but just couldn't place her. She listened very intently to my tale. A positive emotional quality between us seemed to be mutual.

A friend of mine came over to us and asked me what had happened. I proceeded to recount my tale in Hebrew, as he understood that language. He tried to impress her by trying to speak in English, and he proceeded to, but rather poorly so. I excused myself politely and left the room. I then proceeded across the hall, and into another room. There, a person I knew (when I woke up, I couldn't quite remember who), was seated behind a table and seemed to be in charge of the contents upon it. On the table was a plate containing a square cake, which was cut into four equal pieces. It was topped with apple and cherry fruit.

I asked the person in charge, as to who might partake of the cake. He replied with a list of names, and my name was mentioned among them. Then I awoke.

1) The wide open meadow with the sun shining - Comfortable living.

2) The forest dense - Difficulties and problems in life that must be hurdled and travelled through. The trees are one's obstacles.

3) The path ascending - The Torah's path as one's guide through the forest of life's problems.

4) The abyss - Gehinnom.

5) The Clouds of Mist - Heaven (Gan Eden).

6) The Rainbow - The covenant as a reminder to repent from one's sins.

7) The Sun's setting - The day is short, but the work is great. There is very little time left. Come back on the path of Torah and descend with it (humble yourself). (Keep in mind that I was having this dream on the eve of Rosh Chodesh, to prompt me to prepare for Rosh Chodesh teshuvah.)

8) Total darkness in the forest - The suffering for one's sins, as this is the medicine which contributes to the atonement for one's sins. Total despair but...

9) The tiny ray of light - The sparkle of hope. Bitachon. Hashem has shown you the way out, by means of the Torah light.

10) The meadow again - You have attained the level of forgiveness. You breathe comfortably.

11) Dusk - But there is still to do before the sun is completely gone and night falls.

12) The house in the meadow - You must proceed to it. The house is the wife.

13) The window brightly lit, the lights are on inside - Yes, it is the house which is brightly lit, that I must enter. A wife lights the candles; she lights up her home. The Talmud teaches: "A wife is the light of his eyes."

14) Enter and recount my story - I tell of my encounter with Hashem's grace, and praise Him to all the people.

15) The girl - A mutual desire for marriage.

16) The boy - E. Cohen. He was the boy in the dream. Within the year, he introduced me to my future wife!

17) The Man with the cake - In charge of handing out *zivugim*.

18) My name mentioned among the numerous names - My eligibility and merit to marry my *zivug*.

Note the eighteen points of the dream. The Mishnah states: "Eighteen for marriage."

Marriage often constitutes the will of a dream. The mysterious forest of Amukah – a hidden valley of mystical dreams.

Chapter Seventeen

Settling Down Near Amukah

One late Shabbos afternoon in the Lakewood Yeshivah dining room, I was having a cup of tea. Seated across the table from me were two young lads.

"Tell us," one of them said to me, "you've just gotten back from Eretz Yisroel. Please tell us about the Holy Land."

They sat mesmerized, for over an hour, as I recounted and reminisced about my experiences there, during my yeshivah stay.

"We're moving to Eretz Yisroel next month," one of the young lads remarked.

"Really. That's most fortunate!"

"And my friend here; his family will be moving there several months after mine."

"What's your name?"

"Shmuly."

"How old are you?"

"Ten."

"Your're lucky to be moving to Eretz Yisroel. How I wish I could join you and settle down in the Holy Land!"

* * *

More than a year later...

"Mazel Tov!"

Our wedding took place in Yerushalayim. We couldn't afford the high rents there for more than three months, so my wife and I decided to set our sights on Tzefas. Posters all over town advertised Tzefas as having the cheapest rents and purchase prices for apartments, in the entire country.

The first Shabbos in Tzefas, we were invited to be the guests at the table of a quaint family, originally from Lakewood.

At the table, I couldn't help but notice that I recognized one of the faces from somewhere. Their son. He looked familiar. Where had I seen him before? And he was looking at me rather inquisitively too.

"Your boy. His face looks so familiar. I know I must have seen him before. But where?"

Then their son interjected, "Now I remember you. My friend and I sat with you in the Lakewood Yeshivah dining room, one Shabbos afternoon, and you told us all about Eretz Yisroel. It was about a month before we moved here."

"Yes...yes, now I remember. Your name is..."

"Shmuly."

"What a small world! And do you remember what I told you when you mentioned you would be moving to Eretz Yisroel?"

"That you wished you could be joining us."

"That's right! And here I am! At your table!"

Shmuly's father and I became *chavrusos*, and we have been so for the last nine years.

I never dreamt that I would actually settle down in Eretz Yisroel, much less Tzefas.

Indeed, little did I dream that I would one day settle down near Amukah - Amukah the hidden valley. A hidden valley of mystical dreams.

THE END